playing
with icons

JOHN PRIDMORE

The Spirituality of Recalled Childhood

Foreword by
Jerome W. Berryman

ISBN 978-0-692-83985-0

For my wife Pat who, in person or in spirit, has been
at my side throughout this endeavour. Pat's own work
with and for children, especially in the poor places
of the world, is a shining light. If there is anything
worthwhile in what follows, it is because some of that
light has fallen on these pages.

CONTENTS

FOREWORD

When we think of icons we usually think of *praying* with them. Then along comes John Pridmore to suggest that *playing* with icons is a kind of prayer. Icons are usually thought of as images painted on wood, primarily of Jesus and Mary, to help us be aware of God's presence. As we look at them, they look past us at God to remind us that God is looking at us. This book asserts that when we play with children God joins in the game.

Thinking of children as icons of God fits nicely with Jesus' saying that we need to become like children to enter God's kingdom. Jesus went further. He also said that when we welcome children, which is the only way we can know what they are like, we also welcome him and the *one* who sent him (Matthew 18:1-5; Mark 9:36-37 and Mark 10:15; Luke 9:46-48 and Luke 18:17). When we welcome children they reveal God and God's kingdom to us like icons.

John Pridmore was a child during World War II. He lived in "bomb-alley," listening for German "doodlebugs" guttering to a stop in the sky above Sidcup, a suburban district of south-east London, and falling into the homes below to blow up his small world. Later during the tense Cold War days in Berlin he was a corporal in the Intelligence Corps. He wrote casually about this, "Once I was a soldier in Berlin. On Sundays, when I wasn't soldering, I ran a Sunday School."[1] He had not forgotten what it was like to be a child in a devastated neighborhood.

After Berlin he graduated from Nottingham University and trained to be an Anglican priest at Ridley Hall, Cambridge. John served his title in the parish of Camborne, in the county of Cornwall, 'whose paths are worn by angels' feet'.[2] John returned to Ridley Hall as Chaplain and Tutor, then he moved to King Edward's School, Witley from 1971-1986 in the

---

1   John Pridmore, *The Word Is Very Near You: Feasts and Festivals* (Norwich: Canterbury Press, 2010) 1-4.

2   John Pridmore, *The Inner City of God: The Diary of an East End Parson* (Norwich: Canterbury Press, 2008) 12.

wooded hills of Surrey southwest of London. After this he served the International School Moshi in Tanzania, which was located in an "absurdly beautiful location" on the slopes of Mount Kilimanjaro. In 1995 he was appointed as one of the curates at St. Martin-in-the-Fields on London's Trafalgar Square for five years and then he moved to London's East End where he served the Church of St. John-at-Hackney for eleven years. He told this rollicking and deeply moving story in *The Inner-City of God: The Diary of an East End Parson*. In 2009 he published *The Word Is Very Near You* concerning the readings for Sundays in the lectionary and a second volume appeared the next year concerning feasts and festivals that do not fall on Sunday. Both were gathered from his essays in the *Church Times* over several years.

Along the way, John wrote an M.A. thesis in 1967 about what the Hebrew and Christian Scriptures had to say about children. He stayed close to the original languages to do this. He wanted to remind himself and all of us about what the Bible actually said in its own way concerning children. This was published in Australia in 1977 as the text for a conference about children and the church. This was also foundational for *Playing with Icons*.

In 2000 John finished his Ph.D. Thesis for the Institute of Education at the University of London with the encouragement and support of his wife Pat. He dedicated it "to the children of Hackney" with loving mention of his and Pat's daughter Rebecca. The Thesis was about George MacDonald (1824-1905) with special emphasis on his fantasy writing and how it can contribute to our "transfiguration." In thesis language the beauty and breadth of transfiguration was called "spiritual development."

MacDonald mentored Lewis Carroll and encouraged him to publish *Alice in Wonderland*, which had been read aloud to the many children in the MacDonald household. MacDonald's influence can be seen in many English authors such as C. S. Lewis, Tolkien, and Walter del la Mare as well as the Americans Mark Twain, who became a friend, and more recently Madeleine L'Engle. A concise and graceful version of the Thesis may be found in the article "George MacDonald's Estimate of Childhood," which was published in the *International Journal of Children's Spirituality*.[3]

---

3   John Pridmore, "George MacDonald's Estimate of Childhood" in *International Journal of Children's Spirituality* (Volume 12, Number 1, April 2007) 61-74.

There is much more that could be said to introduce you to John Pridmore, but this is enough to suggest that his judgment is sound and his care with texts and people profound. He came twice from England to the Center for the Theology of Childhood in Denver to study, as he was preparing this manuscript. His book is the first in a series to be produced by the Center about children, their spirituality, and their religion. It was a delight to have him busy in the library at the Center and our laughter shook the books as we talked.

To further set the stage for *Playing with Icons* I would like to mention two other very significant books from England about children's spirituality, written during the last forty years. Each of these three books approached the subject from a different angle, which makes their combined insight especially interesting.

Edward Robinson's *The Original Vision* in 1977 was based on a study done at what was then called the Religious Experience Research Unit (RERU) at Manchester College, Oxford. The study involved the memories of adults about their childhood experiences of God's presence.

Sir Alister Hardy, the founder of RERU, invited all those who "felt that their lives had in any way been affected by some power beyond themselves" to write an "account" of the experience and the effect it had them. Robinson wrote concerning the study, "No mention was made of childhood; nevertheless some 15% of all our correspondents (they now number over 4,000) started by going back to events and experiences of their earliest years."[4]

He followed up on about 500 reports about childhood and got detailed responses from "360 or so correspondents." As he poured over the accounts he concluded "the original vision" we have in our early years "is no mere imaginative fantasy but a form of *knowledge* and one that is essential to the development of any mature understanding." This kind of knowing is kin to mystical experience and is natural. These experiences are "self-authenticating" in two senses. Their significance carries its own authority and this self-authentication contributes to the knowledge of the self.[5]

---

4   Edward Robinson, *The Original Vision* (Oxford: The Religious Experience Research Unit, Manchester College, 1977) 11.

5   *The Original Vision*, 16.

Robinson's book liberally quotes from the accounts to build up a rich and layered sense of what the original vision is like and to respect the uniqueness of each account. The original vision is not a deficiency when compared to adults, as Piaget inferred. It is a reality upon which our adult wholeness is built.

The knowing of childhood matures across the decades. When it is inhibited or lost in adulthood our maturity is diminished. This is why "childhood," as a way of knowing, can't be understood by only looking at children. Robinson concluded by saying that "The great majority of those whose experience led me to make this study are men and women in whom the original vision of childhood has never wholly faded. But are they typical? And what of the rest of us who have no such memories? 'If the child within me dies a little more each day, how,' asks Marcel, 'am I to be faithful to myself?' And when I cannot do this, 'I am no longer there. I do not exist any more'."[6]

The Spirit of the Child by the late David Hay with Rebecca Nye is the second book I would like to use to provide the context for *Playing with Icons*. Hay provided the rationale for the empirical study done by Dr. Nye, a child psychologist, who wrote the two "central" chapters[7] in the book. Her conversations with children in two English primary schools probed what children understand about their spirituality *while they are still children*. This is a remarkable piece of work because, as heard over and over again in the accounts of Robinson's study, children don't often tell adults about their experiences of God. They feel adults will not understand. In this case the children found that Rebecca Nye was someone who did understand and was someone they could trust to talk to about such things.

The study involved three meetings with each of thirty-eight children from six to eleven years. The 1,000 typed pages of the interviews were the basis for Nye's discovery that children this age have a sense of their own

---

6   *The Original Vision*, 148. Gabriel Marcel (1889-1973) was a French existen-
    tialist philosopher interested in such themes as creative fidelity and mystery.

7   David Hay with Rebecca Nye, *The Spirit of the Child*, Revised Edition
    (London: Jessica Kingsley Publishers, 2006). HarperCollins published
    an earlier version of this book in 1998. Nye's two chapters, however, are
    virtually unchanged.

spirituality, which she called "relational consciousness." They were aware of and valued the *relations* they had with others, with God, with the environment, and with themselves. Their spirituality was not here nor there but in the creative energy of the in-between.

The elaborate categories of "awareness-sensing," "mystery-sensing," and "value-sensing" that were developed in advance of the conversations to guide them missed the mark. Hay wrote, the word "relationship" did "not even appear as one of the sub-categories of spiritual awareness in our first attempt to give a specification that would be usable in talking to children." This missing of the mark is what gave Hay and Nye their confidence in the value of their study. The conclusion emerged from the data, not their hypothesis.[8]

Playing with Icons provides a different but related point of view. The first difference is that John Pridmore took the relatively unexplored route of studying "writers of published autobiographies of childhood." This was because "no one told them what to tell us." They used their sensitivities and art as authors to probe what it is like to be a child from their own unique points of view.[9] He wrote, "Our best autobiographies of childhood, however much they invent, tell a true story. A tray of fragments can never do that. So a sequel to this present essay could well be a study of autobiographical novels of childhood, beginning with David Copperfield."[10] This suggestion picks up Edward Robinson's idea that the kind of knowledge our original vision involves needs to be studied as it develops through the decades of adulthood to fully understand it.

While reading countless "memoirs of childhood" it became clear to the author that we are spiritual before we are religious and that there is "much macabre and lifeless religion that shows little evidence of the spiritual."[11] He wrote, "My emphasis in this study is on transcendence—on self-transcendence rather than on self-discovery and self-awareness."[12] There is a continuum of spiritual awareness and related moral awareness.

---

8   *The Spirit of the Child*, 131-132.

9   John Pridmore, *Playing with Icons* (Denver: Center for the Theology of Childhood of the Godly Play Foundation, 2017) 22.

10 *Playing with Icons*, 32.

11 *Playing with Icons*, 16.

12 *Playing with Icons*, 26.

Pridmore's image of the extremes in this continuum was that while William Blake may have seen angels in apple-trees, a boy standing next to him might see only apples.

This brings us to another difference between *Playing with Icons* and the two context setting studies. *Playing with Icons* uses Christian language more freely. Two modest examples will suffice. John Pridmore agreed with the view of Frank Kendon in *The Small Years* that, "to disclose the secret of childhood is to unfold the mystery of the incarnation. ... Perhaps it is not entirely farfetched to suggest that to revisit childhood is to engage with the Word made flesh. We shall at least be open to that possibility."[13]

A second example was suggested in passing, "somewhat mischievously." It is a child-sensitive comment about scripture. Pridmore observed that St. Paul wrote to the Christians in Rome, "I was once alive... (Romans 7:9)." Was this a reference to his childhood before he became involved with trying to live properly by the law of Moses?

The comments by publishers about John Pridmore's book are interesting. One American publisher thought the text was too English for publication in America. An English publisher thought the autobiographies Pridmore studied were too outdated for the contemporary English reader. After lengthy discussion the author concluded, "I would argue that the continuities between the lives of the children we have met in this study and the lives of contemporary children are more significant than the discontinuities, notable as they are."[14] "Remembering childhood, it seems, is like describing the paradoxical behaviour of light. Like light, recalled childhood is at once a succession of myriad particles and one unbroken wave."[15] It is in the unbroken wave, it seems to me, that the continuities swell.

My sense is that the foundational texts for Pridmore's book are universal and timeless, despite the limitations of when and where they were written, which makes this the kind of book that the Center for the Theology of Childhood is interested in publishing. Sometimes one needs to be warmly open to the subject matter of children's spirituality and

---

13   *Playing with Icons*, 22.
14   *Playing with Icons*, 186.
15   *Playing with Icons*, 30.

patient in one's reading to take in what a book like this has to offer. This becomes abundantly clear with a second reading.

John Pridmore did not write to express a thesis he held in advance. He wrote to "wrestle with the angel of childhood" in Frank Kendon's words. We are invited to join him to explore children's intensity and immediacy, their capacity to see beyond, their inward pain of spiritual distress, their ability to hear the silences in nature, their heightened awareness of what transcends the ordinary, their intuition about the negative and positive influences of religion, and, finally to explore what they disclose about the child we are called to become to enter God's kingdom.

This book is intended to be an existential journey, as the author makes plain in the very first chapter. We are invited to play with and welcome the *verbal* icons in this book and the running and laughing ones we know around us and in our own memories, so they can reveal themselves and the One who shines through them to "transfigure" us.[16]

---

16 John Pridmore wrote in his Thesis (page 160) that MacDonald's fantasy is transfiguring. It subverts "the distinction by which we ordinarily order and contain our experience, above all the boundary between the texts we read and the lives we lead. Our spiritual development is promoted as we work out the sequel and discover the meaningful pattern of the unclosed narrative we put down in the lives we take up." Perhaps, this idea can be extended to reading autobiographies of childhood about unfinished adult lives. We need to finish them with the living of our days.

PREFACE

Frank Kendon, poet and pacifist, born in 1893, grew up in a hamlet on a hill in the weald of Kent. It was, he tells us, 'a kindly piece of England to be cradled in'. He was the son of the headmaster of a little boarding school for boys. Later in life he wrote a beautiful book about what was in many ways an idyllic childhood, a memoir he entitled *The Small Years*. Kendon tells us why he writes about the boy he was. It is 'to wrestle with the angel of childhood till he tells me his secret, and then . . . to put that down, truthfully, for a particular addition to the joy of the world' (Kendon, 1950, 161).

This essay, *Playing with Icons*, is a study of memoirs of childhood such as Frank Kendon's. I turn to these memoirs with the same purpose that prompted Kendon to revisit his own childhood. My aim too is 'to wrestle with the angel of childhood'. As Kendon did, I ask what it is to be a child and I look for light on that question in what he and other writers recall of their early years.

So that is my question. What is it to be a child? And I go to some of the many who have written about their own childhoods to help me engage with it. Of course there are many other ways to approach childhood. 'Childhood studies' embrace numerous disciplines—sociological, historical, psychological, and the rest—but the route I have chosen remains relatively unexplored.

To enquire what it is to be a child is to ask about what we have come to call 'children's spirituality', a topic that has attracted much attention in recent years. 'Spirituality' is a slippery and contested concept and soon I shall have more to say about what I mean by it. Suffice it to say for the moment that I shall propose, using a broad brush, that our spirituality is that in us that reaches to 'the other and the beyond'.

A basic premise of this study is that from our birth—and indeed from before our birth—we are spiritual beings, however elusive that idea proves to be. A further premise is that our spirituality is a fact about us whether or not we choose to explain it in religious terms. The truth of the claim that *homo sapiens sapiens* is a spiritual creature is no doubt required by a religious view of life, but it is not the case that spirituality needs religion to thrive. We are spiritual before we are religious. To be sure religion needs spirituality if it is to ring true. There is, alas, much macabre and lifeless religion that shows little evidence of the spiritual, as what follows will show. But spirituality does not require religion to flourish and we shall meet many spirited children in these pages who manage without it—or despite it.

I stress that we can study the spirit of the child without using a religious framework. That said, those within the Christian tradition will have particular and compelling reasons to try to understand children and childhood. Children mattered to Jesus. It follows that those who seek to be open to the spirit of Jesus are bound to be attentive to children. They will try both to learn about children and to learn from children. They will seek too to nurture the spirit of children—whether their own children or those entrusted to them in school or church. More will be said in our first chapter about these specifically Christian grounds for studying the spirituality of childhood.

I seek to make better sense of what it is to be a child and of what is required if children are to flourish spiritually. That is my quest as I look back with our writers on their childhoods. Anyone who finds such a quest worthwhile is the one I am writing for.

Memories of childhood are no easier to control and organise than children themselves. But an attempt must be made to discern recurring themes and to present our material in some sort of order. A problem immediately looms. So rich are the texts we are reviewing in our search for an understanding of the spirit of the child, that we would have little difficulty in finding in them whatever we decide in advance must be there. We come to these texts with our already settled assumptions. The risk is that our study becomes no more than a hunt for evidence to support conclusions already made. Nevertheless certain themes are sufficiently common to our memoirs to allow me to hope that I am not simply selecting from them what I want them to say. Clearly these recurrent themes overlap, but they are sufficiently distinct to be treated in turn.

In our first chapter I shall say more about the approach adopted in this study, touching on some of the difficulties an investigation of this kind raises. Not least we have to ask, given that memory is such an unreliable instrument, whether the memories we canvass are to be trusted.

In Chapter Two we meet the children who our writers once were and notice the intensity and immediacy of their perceptions. We join most of these children when they were very young. We shall register what might be described as the 'spirited senses' of these younger children. What to the adult is commonplace and familiar is perceived by the child in its true light as something remarkable. That everyday object, as so it seems to the grown-up, is to the child what the New Testament calls a *thaumasion*—'a wonderful thing'. The child's 'primal vision' allows him or her to see as rarely they will see again. But it is not sight alone that is spirited. So it is with all the senses—not least the sense of smell. The child I must become and the child whose path to God in Christ I must make plain is acutely attentive to the sensed 'there-ness' of things.

The theme of Chapter Three is the capacity of children to 'see beyond'. Children see what is there and see it for what it is. But many of our memoirs suggest that they also see what many sceptical adults would insist is *not* there—and that they see too *those* who are not there, at least to the adult eye. Some children have invisible companions, no less real to them than their siblings at home or their friends at school. So we turn from children's perception of what both old and young agree is there, however unappreciative we grown-ups are of it, to the child's awareness— or imaginative creation—of what is beyond appearances.

'Lord, give to men who are old and tougher/ The things that little children suffer'. So wrote, so prayed, John Masefield in *The Everlasting Mercy*. To speak of the spirit of the child is to refer to who he or she ultimately is. No attribute is more fundamental to the child's identity, so our memoirs suggest, than the child's capacity to suffer. Children hurt— and memories of their suffered hurt are the theme of our fourth chapter. In a more wide-ranging study than this, proper place would have to be made for physical and material suffering of children, especially in the poor places of our world. Here the suffering on which we focus is inward pain, what we have come to call 'spiritual distress'. If children are not yet able to distance themselves from that inner anguish, if as yet they have 'no language but a cry', then that pain is all the more grievous. Toddlers as well as saints, I shall suggest, experience the dark night of the soul.

William Wordsworth is at our shoulder throughout this study. He wrote of the child he was, the boy who roamed the Cumberland hills and lakesides, the boy to whose heart the voice—and, still more, the silences— of nature spoke. Many other writers recall how the natural world furnished, enriched, and shaped their childhood and I turn to them in Chapter Five. Ours is an urbanised technological age in which few children go out to play. We are bound to fear that such children are spiritually malnourished.

'For most of us, there is only the unattended/ Moment, the moment in and out of time . . .' That is how T. S. Eliot describes, in his *Four Quartets*, those occasions of heightened awareness, transcending ordinary experience and resisting explanation, which momentarily but marvellously interrupt the usual humdrum tenor of our days. Many claim that such 'unattended moments' can be sufficiently accounted for in psychological terms and rule out the possibility that they might betoken a greater reality. I do not accept this reductionist view. I refuse to discount the possibility that these rare moments are evidential. Children are often shy of talking about such experiences. Sometimes we hear about them only when those children have become adults and break their silence. They do so in the texts to which I turn in Chapter Six.

Central to this study is the contentious question of the relationship of spirituality and religion. Does spirituality require religion if it is to be more than a misty mood? Or can we flourish spiritually just as well, if not better, without religion? Most of the children we shall meet had some experience of formal religion. For some that experience is suffocating, threatening to stifle their spiritual growth, or simply inadequate, failing sufficiently to express all that most moves them. I discuss their painful memories in Chapter Seven. For others, for those whose recollections we look at in Chapter Eight, religion promotes their spirituality, above all lending them a language with which to utter what lies beyond words. I shall suggest that the reason why religion should oppress the spirit of one child and set another child's spirit soaring has all to do with which face, frowning or smiling, we grown-ups turn on them.

Religion lends a language. It is the supreme gift of religion to the spirit. This principle will prove to be of the first importance as our study unfolds. We stay with this theme in our ninth chapter. Opinions may differ as to whether or not children's spirituality can be articulated and promoted only within a received religious tradition. But there can be little disagreement that spirituality seeks to express itself. The spirit answers to words and music, and in words and music the spirit finds her voice. Our writers tell us how stories and songs spoke to them as children. So too—at least to some of them—did the language of liturgy and scripture, of hymns and sacred music, whether or not those children grew up to be religious believers.

In our tenth and final chapter I try to summarise what we have learned from our memoirs about the spirit of the child. That summary will be a less a record of new discoveries—though we are in for at least some surprises—than an overview of a landscape seen from a perspective rarely taken. We shall see that, from our fresh perspective, certain features of the landscape stand out more conspicuously than from the more familiar vantage points from which childhood has generally been observed. This project will have been worthwhile if, from its eccentric viewpoint, it helps me to understand a little better the child I once was, the child I must nurture, and the child I must become.

***

I eagerly acknowledge the debt I owe to Dr Jerome Berryman, the creator of Godly Play, who made this project possible. I am deeply grateful to Jerome, first, for his encouraging me to see memoirs of childhood as a worthwhile field of study; secondly, for his great generosity in welcoming me to work with him at his Centre for the Theology of Childhood in Denver, Colorado; and, thirdly, for his many insights which are reflected, if not sufficiently attributed, in this study. I hope that my engagement with the life-stories discussed in these pages reflects, in however small measure, the wisdom of the approach of Godly Play to a greater story still.

I am much indebted to the Ms W. Lee Dickson MBA, Executive Director of the Godly Play Foundation and the Revd Dr Cheryl Minor, Director of the Center for the Theology of Childhood, for their patience with an author bewildered by the challenges of getting a text ready for publication. They went more than the extra mile in preparing this little book to see the light of day and I am most grateful to them.

I would also like to thank Tanja Havemann for her kind permission to use the drawing on the back cover.

John Pridmore
2017

CHAPTER 1

WRESTLING WITH THE ANGEL OF CHILDHOOD

Frank Kendon's purpose in writing about his boyhood was 'to wrestle with the angel of childhood'. Many who ask what it is to be a child have no distinctively Christian reason for doing so. Children make us wonder who they are whether or not we are Christians. But, as a Christian of sorts, I do have at least three particular reasons for putting that question.

I ask the question, first, because I am haunted by the words of one who tells me that, unless I become as a little child, I shall not enter the kingdom of God (Matthew 18.3). Surely I must know who this child is, if I am to shape my life after his or her likeness.

Still sterner words give me my second reason for asking what it means to be a child. Jesus warns me that if I 'cause a child to stumble' it would better for me if a millstone were hung round my neck and I were drowned in the depths of the sea' (Matthew 18.6). To 'cause a child to stumble' is simply to put some obstacle in the child's path, making it difficult or impossible for him or her to come to Jesus. The Jesus we meet in the Gospels was attractive to children. The Jesus children meet in church is less so. That is because we misrepresent him or surround him with so much clutter that the child can scarcely catch a glimpse of him. (God is often even less attractive to children than Jesus. We shall notice in due course the distinction children draw between the two.)

If we want children to flourish within the Christian family, they need a true picture of Jesus, although even our best attempt at one is bound to be a poor likeness. As an adult, I may find my image of Jesus compelling, but if the picture that pleases me repels the child, or does not make sense to the child, it is a false image. It follows that I must 'wrestle with the angel of childhood' until that angel tells me the secret of how children *perceive*.

Perhaps then the image of Jesus—or of God—I offer them may not be such a grotesque caricature.

My third reason for pressing the question 'Who is the child?' is that it I find it merging with another question, the most important any of us can ask—'Who is this man?' Frank Kendon recognises this deeper dimension to the quest for childhood. With a boldness bordering on audacity, he sets these words from the Bible at the beginning of his book.

'That which from the beginning, which we have heard, which we have seen with our eyes, which we have looked upon, and our hands have handled of the word of life. For the life was manifested, and we have seen it, and bear witness' (1 John 1.1).

It is an astonishing epigraph to a book which might seem much like many another affectionate memoir of a distant childhood. Searching for the secret of one's childhood is, it seems, sacred work. Frank Kendon suggests that to disclose the secret of childhood is to unfold the mystery of the incarnation. We protest at such an absurd proposal—until, that is, we recall the words of Jesus: 'Whoever receives a child in my name receives me' (Mark 9.37). Perhaps it is not entirely far-fetched to suggest that to revisit childhood is to engage with the Word made flesh. We shall at least be open to that possibility in the pages that follow, not least as we turn to accounts of afflicted childhoods.

My childhood is a mysterious realm which does not yield its secrets lightly. Henry Vaughan is conscious of the sheer inaccessibility of childhood:

'I cannot reach it; and my striving eye
Dazzles at it, as at eternity' (*Childhood*).

Childhood belongs to my past, to the foreign country where, famously, 'they do things differently'. So I shall need all the help I can get to explore it. Child psychologists, for example, know that country well and I would be foolish to ignore them. But they will not be my guides in my present quest. I turn to others and follow a different path, an approach that, so far as I know, has not been taken previously in reflecting on the Christian significance of childhood.

I turn to writers of published autobiographies of childhood, such as Frank Kendon, to help me understand what it is to be a child. These memoirs are a rich resource. They are windows into a world we must re-enter if we believe that the child is to be the pattern of our discipleship and that we imperil our salvation if we cause a child to stumble.

Not all who write about their childhood think about what they are doing as carefully as Kendon does. The consequence is that most memoirs of childhood are not really about childhood at all. Rather, they are social studies, essays in local history describing the customs and characters of the worlds—the family, the school, the church, and so on—where the child grew up. Mary Lakeman's *Early Tide: A Mevagissey childhood* (Lakeman, 1978), for example, tells us much about the delightful Cornish fishing village of Mevagissey but little about young Mary. Such accounts are often fascinating and they are rich in material for social historians. But they do not engage with the question of what it means to be a child. Virginia Woolf, who read everything, read many childhood memoirs. She dismissed most of them as failures. 'They leave out the person to whom things happened... They say: "This is what happened" but they do not say what the person was like to whom things happened' (*Woolf*, 1989, 73). Such books do not help me to become the child Christ wants me to be. Nor do they help me to nurture children in faith and love.

In this study I shall stay with writers who, like Frank Kendon, have heard the question, 'What is it to be a child?' and I shall disregard the memoirs, much as I have enjoyed many of them, which do not ask that question. My interest is in those writers who seek to *understand* their childhood. So we won't follow little Mary Lakeman down the back lanes of Mevagissey. Given our priorities, I make no apology for returning to a number of memoirs repeatedly. These will include the classical accounts of childhood by the great Russian writers, notably those of Serghei Aksakoff, Elisaveta Fen, Maxim Gorky, Konstantin Paustovsky, and Leo Tolstoy. There are others, less illustrious, who relive their childhoods in autobiographies which I revisit repeatedly. Together these writers have bequeathed to us what we might call the canonical accounts of childhood. Unlike the Bible, this canon can always accommodate more titles as we come across them or as they are written. Famous or forgotten, these authors will be our companions and guides.

Why make *writers* our companions? We do so because they speak. They are blessed with a voice. Most of us struggle for words to capture what we experienced as children. But writers find words. It is what they do. It is what they are good at. They articulate the experiences, for which most of us, whether children or adults, have 'no language but a cry'. Among them there are some few writers—those who have bequeathed to us their 'canonical' accounts of childhood—who identify so closely with the child they once were and who speak so well for him or her, that they become that child again. Only the tongue, the pen, the keyboard, is the adult's.

A further powerful reason for turning to these writers is that no one told them what to tell us. They were not being asked research questions which, however carefully phrased, were bound to be loaded. No one, armed with clip-board or tape-recorder, disturbed them at their task.

Others have studied memoirs of childhood. Much the weightiest of these studies is Richard Coe's *When the Grass was Taller* (Coe, 1984), a magisterial work based on the author's reading of some six hundred of them. I gladly acknowledge my debt to Richard Coe's great book, but this study is narrower than his and not only because I cannot move to and fro between half a dozen European languages as readily as he does. We turn to our memoirs with a particular interest and a specific question. We search these texts for what they tell us—in one word instead of dozens more—about the 'spirituality' of the child.

The spirituality of childhood

The meaning of 'spirituality' is the subject of much debate, a debate fed from two sources. First, there is the proliferation of paths to which many now turn in preference to those of traditional religion. Some of these alternative 'spiritualities' draw from ancient springs. Others, more or less crackpot, are no older than the day before yesterday. Secondly, since 1944, the promotion of 'spiritual development' has been a curricular requirement in state-funded schools in England and Wales. Today teachers of every subject, not only of religious education, must make sure that their lessons contribute to the spiritual flourishing of their students. Understandably, teachers ask what exactly is expected of them by this mandatory requirement.

The maths teacher's terror mounts as she notices the OFSTED inspector at the back of the classroom, his pencil poised to note whether or not her lesson on equilateral triangles is promoting the spiritual welfare of her Year Seven pupils.

For all the talk about what it means, the term 'spiritual' continues to defy definition. G. K. Chesterton, in characteristically robust fashion, tells us that in worrying about how such a word is to be defined, we are creating a problem where none exists.

'Much of our modern difficulty, in religion and other things, arises merely from this: that we confuse the word "indefinable" with the word "vague". If someone speaks of a spiritual fact as "indefinable" we promptly picture something misty, a cloud with indeterminate edges. But this is an error even in commonplace logic. The thing that cannot be defined is the first thing; the primary fact. It is our arms and legs, our pots and pans that are indefinable. The indefinable is the indisputable. The man next door is indefinable, because he is too actual to be defined. And there are some to whom spiritual things have the same fierce and practical proximity; some to whom God is too actual to be defined' (Chesterton, 2007, 3).

'The indefinable is the indisputable.' Spirituality escapes definition, as do such concepts of 'goodness' and 'love'. But what cannot be defined can be recognised and described. For years I have worked with a broad-brush description of spirituality—a description, not a definition—that has served tolerably well. Our spirituality, I suggest, is 'our awareness of the other and the beyond'. Such awareness is not illusory. It is an innate dimension of our human nature. It is how we are. Here is not the place to defend that claim. That has been well done elsewhere, notably by David Hay in his study of 'the biology of the human spirit' entitled *Something There* (Hay, 2006). Sadly, we are shy of speaking of the spiritual. Deep down we are well aware that there is indeed 'something there', but we are strangely reluctant to tell of what we know. We fear that others would not understand what we are talking about. When we are small we will be afraid that other boys and girls will make fun of us. In reality experiences of 'the other and the beyond' are far from rare. Most people, when gently asked whether there have been occasions when they were touched by the transcendent, will own to them. An archive of thousands of such responses is held by the Religious Experience Research Centre of the University of Wales (*www. uwtsd.ac.uk/library/alister-hardy-religious-experience-research-centre*).

The description of spirituality I have elected to work with—choosing it rather than one of the many others that have been proposed—discloses an emphasis in my approach that some students of spirituality may feel is out of kilter. My emphasis in this study is on transcendence—on self-transcendence rather than on self-discovery and self-awareness. Questions of the self certainly trouble the child. Bryan Magee, for example, who grew up to be a philosopher, was already perplexed as a child by the problem of who he was (*Magee*, 2004, 210-211). The novelist and science-fiction writer Colin Middleton Murry describes the moment when he became aware of his 'self'—'or, rather,' he writes, 'I became aware of a self that had its lodging within my body and now peered out at the world through the bleared windows that were my eyes' (Murry, 1975, 14). Awareness of self and a sense of security of self—comfort in one's own skin, so to speak—are indeed spiritual issues. If these issues are not fully explored in this essay, that does not mean that further investigation in our field would not throw light on them.

Perhaps here is the point to acknowledge that there are other important aspects of children's spirituality which are not discussed in this brief study. For example, I do not directly address the question of whether autobiographies of childhood indicate that the spiritual perceptions of boys and girls differ significantly. That is a question that invites and deserves further study.

We might ask too whether our memoirs show that the experience of 'sickness' and 'disability' in childhood shapes a child's spiritual awareness. (The inverted commas embrace two words that, of course, require much unpacking.) We shall soon meet an aristocratic Russian child whose recurrent illnesses, so he will claim, led him to live in a private world and, a little later, a blind Egyptian boy for whom the music of the human voice was the voice of God. The broadcaster Peter White alludes to his 'rampant atheism', but he does not suggest that his unbelief had anything to do with his disability (White, 1999, 111). Our encounters with such children suggest that there are links to be explored another time between illness and impairment and spiritual awareness. The extended study such an exploration would merit might well begin with a close reading of Karl Bjarnhof's *The Stars Grow Pale*. Bjarnhof, a Danish musician and—like Peter White—a broadcaster, slowly lost his sight during his childhood. His memoir, a poignant record of how religion can fail to keep pace with the spirit, is among the most moving I have read (Bjarnhof, 1960).

The spiritual is an aspect of our nature. It is there from the start. Extensive empirical research among children, such as the investigation into the core of children's spirituality conducted by David Hay and Rebecca Nye (Hay and Nye, 1998) has provided evidence that this is so. The memories we turn to in this book will be further testimony to this fundamental truth about us, that from our earliest days the spiritual is an inalienable dimension of our humanity.

To claim that our spirituality is, as we sometimes say, 'hard-wired' into us is not to say that spiritual awareness, any more than any other faculty, is equally acute in everyone. Human beings are all musical, but not everyone has an ear for music. Frances Donaldson, daughter of snobbish gentry, recalls: 'We were completely unimaginative children, never indulging in fantasy, and, I speak here for myself, without any interior life'. She remembers an occasion when Daphne du Maurier made them all play Roundheads and Cavaliers. 'It was the only imaginative game I ever remember playing,' she tells us, 'and I did not enjoy it' (Donaldson, 1959, 27).

It does not help to speculate whether all along there were untapped spiritual wells within such children as little Frances Donaldson. Better to recognise that there is a continuum in spiritual awareness—as we must recognise there is in moral awareness. William Blake saw angels in apple-trees. Perhaps the boy next door only saw apples in them.

The intrusive adult

For all the research on childhood and for all the torrents of literature that research has generated, our earliest years remain largely hidden to us. A curtain has fallen.

Our writers recognise how hard it is to speak truly of their childhood. In his memoir *Far Away and Long Ago*—a text that stands high among our canonical memoirs of childhood—the naturalist W. H. Hudson recalls his growing-up on the vast Argentine pampas. He is aware of the impossibility of recording childhood 'exactly as it was'.

> 'It could not have been what it seems to the adult mind, since we cannot escape from what we are, however great our detachment may be; and in going back we must take our present selves with us' (Hudson, 1931, 225).

Another naturalist, the nineteenth-century writer Richard Jefferies, the 'Bevis' of the wonderful books he wrote about his boyhood, recognises how the adult articulates what the child has neither language nor need to express. 'Bevis, as you know,' he reminds us, 'did not think: we have done the thinking, the analysis for him' (Jefferies, 1932, 356).

When we invade their worlds, the children we once were run away and hide. Elizabeth Hamilton, who writes beautifully about her Anglo-Irish childhood in County Wicklow at the beginning of the twentieth century, is well aware of the perils of her project.

> 'In a sense we create our past. We take events, scenes, persons, dwell upon them, mould them to our purpose, add this, omit that until, like the teller of a story who in part draws upon experience, in part invents, we scarcely know what has objective reality and what has not' (Hamilton, 1963, 13).

Geoffrey Dennis, like Frank Kendon, 'wrestles with the angel of childhood'. His remarkable extended prose-poem *Till Seven* recalls a relatively prosperous Manchester childhood in the late Victorian period. Dennis, now 'naked sixty', says that his purpose in recalling his childhood is 'to yield sole place to the child joined to me by name, by continuity of body and spirit, and mysteriously and alone effectively, by Memory— source and substance of this book'. He admits to how difficult he finds this task. The adult is always intruding. By imposing a pattern on the raw data of the child's experience we privilege our adult interpretation above the child's own testimony.

'The aim is, giving the child, to ban the man. Who yet all the time is restive out of it, champing the bit, chafing at his comparative—oh, most comparative—exclusion, butting in on pretexts of verity or clarity, shedding superfluous sidelights, nosing and glosing' (Dennis, 1957, 137).

Clumsy adults, returning to childhood, 'nose and glose', as Dennis quaintly puts it. To use less idiosyncratic language, they put their grown-up gloss on the child's experience. But some writers are less clumsy than others. Our best guides will be those who know that the child is a timid creature and that he or she must be approached cautiously.

The snapshots and the stream

What do we recall when we remember childhood? For most of us memory's legacy is a sequence of images. 'It is a pure picture world that memory is projecting,' writes Geoffrey Dennis. What we see as we look back are 'separate pictures, as projected on the screen by an old-fashioned magic lantern; not a cinema film unrolled in continuity' (Dennis, 1957, 138).

The adult Konstantin Paustovsky, recalling his childhood in Russia at the turn of the twentieth century, records his memories in a succession of brief paragraphs, many no more than a single sentence. This style—a power-point of sharp snapshots—recognises and captures how the child registers experience as a series of discrete intense impressions (Paustovsky, 1964).

All that remains of her childhood for the novelist Penelope Lively—or for any of us, she claims—is 'a headful of brilliant frozen moments' (Lively, 2006, vii). The self she was, a little girl growing up in Egypt, is irretrievable save for 'such miraculously surviving moments of being'. The example she gives is her recollection of sitting in the back of a car on an outing to Heliopolis. She recalls chanting quietly the names of the trees that line the road: 'Jacaranda, oleander... Jacaranda, oleander...' (Lively, 2006, 1). Many of our memoirs, especially those recalling earliest childhood, are chronicles of such moments. They record what Virginia Woolf describes as 'moments of being' (Woolf, 1989, 87). As we shall see, many such moments may be unremarkable enough in themselves, yet somehow they are charged with significance. Each may prove an example of the 'unattended moment', as T. S. Eliot calls it, where time and the timeless intersect (*Four Quartets*).

Other writers testify to childhood, not so much as a sequence of 'spots of time' to use Wordsworth's term, not as beads on a thread, but rather as a continuous river of experience. Mulk Raj Anand, honoured as 'India's Charles Dickens', writes,

'As I look back upon the first seven years of my own half unconscious and half conscious childhood, I see myself...flowing like a stream, now bright and vivacious with the sunbeams which played upon it, now gloomy with the tears of my sorrow, but always flowing, trickling through the dams and barriers placed in my way, or charging across them so as to demolish them and sweep them aside' (Anand, 2005, 229).

Remembering childhood, it seems, is like describing the paradoxical behaviour of light. Like light, recalled childhood is at once a succession of myriad particles and one unbroken wave. Virginia Woolf embraces this paradox. She speaks of 'the many bright colours; many distinct sounds; some human beings, caricatures, comic; several violent moments of being'. But she adds, 'somehow into that picture must be brought, too, the sense of movement and change. Nothing remained stable long. One must get the feeling of everything approaching and then disappearing' (Woolf, 1989, 88).

As we look back with our writers, it will sometimes be as if we are turning the pages of a photograph album with them. At other times it will be as if we are walking with them beside a river.

The cost of remembering

Recalling childhood is costly. Buried pain must be brought to the surface and re-experienced. Perhaps that is why many of our writers prefer to talk about the world around them rather than about the world within them. It is much easier for me to talk about Mevagissey than it is for me to talk about me. The poet James Kirkup goes as far as to imply that writing about one's childhood requires what Jesus demanded of his disciples. 'To remember one's childhood, he writes, 'we must also become as little children, casting out our prejudice and pride if we are to live our childhood again in a childlike way' (Kirkup, 1957, 13-15).

Kirkup's use of Biblical language resonates with Frank Kendon's. The imagery emboldens us to use other hallowed words to help us grasp what it means to write about a distant childhood. To recall my childhood is to hear and obey a summons from the child I was. That child is telling me, 'Do this in remembrance of me'. Greatly daring, we stay with this sacramental imagery. In some of our memoirs we recognise 'the real presence' of the child. It is as if the author has 're-presented'—made present again—the child they were. In the greatest of our autobiographies of childhood that 'as if' has gone.

Imagination, invention and truth

'Conventional wisdom casts memory as a retrieval system, like a videotape that plays back information that has been recorded onto it, or a computer that accesses the files of what really happened... This model, almost all psychologists would agree, is utter nonsense' (Yagoda, 2009, 103).

Many of our authors appear to remember their childhoods in remarkable detail. Conversations exchanged decades past are recalled word for word. We are bound to wonder whether our writers are relying on exceptional powers of recall or on lively imaginations. Are they making things up? If they are, are they to be trusted? At root is the issue, faced by every historian and biographer, of how we can ever speak truthfully about the past. Authors of autobiography, at least those who think about what they are doing, recognise that to invent is not necessarily to mislead or falsify. Truth is not the same as accuracy and at times may need to dispense with it. What is imagined can often bring the past more truthfully to life than what memory registers or documents corroborate. That is why historical fiction—and, for that matter, the four gospels—can sometimes be better history than the history that never strays beyond verifiable facts. Leslie Stephen, the father of Virginia Woolf, is characteristically caustic. 'An autobiography,' he writes, 'alone of all books, may be more valuable in proportion to the amount of misrepresentation it contains' (Stephen, cited by Yagoda, 111). Our best autobiographies of childhood, however much they invent, tell a true story. A tray of fragments can never do that. So a sequel to this present essay could well be a study of autobiographical novels of childhood, beginning with *David Copperfield*.

Our problem is that we have to make do with the one word 'remember' to refer to two very different tasks memory can undertake. The distinction, unavailable to us in English, is made by two German words, *Gedächtnis* and *Erinnerung*. *Gedächtnis* is the capacity to call to mind when required useful (or, for that matter, useless) information. *Gedächtnis* retrieves the information that two and two make four or that Bogata is the capital of Colombia. *Erinnerung* recalls experience so that in some measure I relive it. Emil Kästner, the much-loved German children's writer, says that his autobiography *Als Ich ein kleines Kind war* (Kästner, 2003) is a work of *Erinnerung*. The memoirs that will interest us in this study are those that record the testimony of *Erinnerung*, of subjective experience recaptured, not those that merely chronicle the impersonal and detached deliverances of *Gedächtnis*.

The lonely child

The obvious must be stated. Our memoirs were written by writers and most people are not writers. Children who go on to write books when they grow up are possibly more sensitive and reflective than other children. If so, it could be said that they are an unrepresentative sample. Certainly, many of our children, on their own admission, were children apart. Richard Coe claims that 'almost without exception, the man or woman who, later in life, returns in imagination to re-visit and recreate a past childhood was, in that childhood, a solitary, alienated, an exceptional child' (Coe, 1984, 51).

Serghei Aksakoff, brought up in a patriarchal Russian family, recalls a crowded household but a solitary childhood. 'Throughout my childhood and for some years later, this peculiarity was noted in me, that I did not make friends with other children'. Alone with himself, he rides an emotional and spiritual roller-coaster, soaring to peaks of manic elation, plunging into paroxysms of grief. The illnesses he was prone to 'brought with them separation and solitude; for such a life forces even a little child back upon himself and confines him to an inner world of his own, which is difficult to share with those who are not in the secret' (Aksakoff, 1923, 145). We shall return repeatedly to Aksakoff's memoir—certainly another of our canonical accounts of childhood.

Mulk Raj Anand remembers his loneliness as a child.

'In the light of those days I am now inclined to think that childhood is not altogether the happy, golden time sentimentalists make it out to be as a compensation for the rigours of the grown-up world, but that it is characterised by long patches of loneliness when children are condemned, for good or ill, to the prison of their own sensibilities.'

Anand looks back with gratitude on his loneliness, but he recognises that there was a price to be paid.

'It is true that the lonely child develops an almost convalescent sensitiveness under these circumstances and creates fantasies for his own delectation, but the burden of this early effort, though profitable in the long run, is heavy to bear when the tender soul has to jump from the dreamy existence of the garden bower to the world of reality which is made up of the parental routine of meals and siestas' (Anand, 2005, 25).

Kathleen Raine, who grew up in a remote Northumberland hamlet and whom we shall get to know better, tells us that, as a child, she had never doubted that she was 'a chosen one'. Her solitariness was not so much that of a lonely child, but rather of a child who does not need other children. 'I had no wish to excel, or to surpass or to be admired; my task concerned no one but myself: the children with whom I played knew nothing of my inner life, in which they played no part' (Raine, 1973, 92).

The poet and critic James Kirkup tells us that from the beginning he was observant, but at the same time 'silent and reserved'. He was, he claims, 'a lonely child' who learned more and more 'to prefer (his) own company to that of other children'. He observes, 'I often began to feel as if I had materialised out of nothing, out of thin air, and that I didn't altogether belong to this world' (Kirkup, 1957, 38).

The poet and story-teller Walter de la Mare would have been drawn to the young Kirkup. Many of the children we shall meet will remind us of de la Mare's lonely introverted children, the children—disturbing, if not disturbed—who figure so frequently in his strange tales, children who, as one critic remarked, 'are just a little odd'.

Should we eliminate such unusual children from our survey? On the contrary, such children are of special interest to us because they can be seen as exhibiting more sharply the lineaments of any child's spirituality. Much as William James, in his *Varieties of Religious Experience*, highlighted unusual or even extreme examples of the patterns of experience he was studying in order to make their distinguishing characteristics more conspicuous, so our 'odd' children are exceptional only in that they show what constitutes the spirit of the child exceptionally clearly. We do not dismiss what poets tell us just because poets are thin on the ground.

Foothills and summits

This book is an exploration of foothills. Our landscape is dominated by a range of summits, accounts of childhood to which we cannot do full justice in a small-scale study. The peaks above us include Henry Vaughan's poems about childhood, Thomas Traherne's *Centuries*, and, above all, the first two books of William Wordsworth's *The Prelude* and Wordsworth's *Ode on the Intimations of Immortality from Recollections of Early Childhood*. Within the boundaries of this study, we cannot discuss such great texts in depth. But neither can we ignore them. The choice I have made is to have these texts to hand as we go along and from time to time to draw attention to the resonances between them and the memoirs I discuss.

Period Piece

There is an urgency to our task. Gwen Raverat, granddaughter of Charles Darwin, grew up in a donnish household in Cambridge at the end of the nineteenth century. She calls the story of her childhood *Period Piece* (Raverat, 1960). Many of our memoirs might have the same title. That is not just because the worlds recalled in some of them—an upstairs-downstairs country-house in Edwardian England, a tenement in the Jewish East End, a Cornish mining village, and the rest—are long gone. It is because childhood itself, many would claim, is fast becoming a period piece. The supreme danger of our days—more threatening than the meltdown of icecaps or economies—is the erosion of childhood.

So at least many commentators in the United Kingdom argue. A letter was published in *The Daily Telegraph* on 24th September 2011, jointly signed by two hundred academics, teachers, authors and charity leaders, in which they said that children's well-being and mental health—what, in shorthand, we are calling their 'spirituality'—is being undermined. British children are sent to school sooner and they spend more time in front of television or computer screens than any other children in Europe. Apart from the hours they spend alone playing computer games—arguably a pursuit less spiritually enriching than games played in the real world with real children—our children are playing less than ever and to the extent that a child ceases to play, that boy or girl ceases to be a child. Each year in the United Kingdom, 'Playday' is celebrated. The purpose of the day is to affirm the fundamental importance of play for children's enjoyment of childhood, and for the vitality of their health, well-being and development. In light of government cuts to play services across the country, the fear of many is that 'Playday' is a campaign for a lost cause. The heart of childhood is still beating, but that heartbeat is faltering.

We 'wrestle with the angel of childhood', till he tells us his secret. We need to know what it means to be a child because the child is the pattern of our discipleship. We need that understanding so as to be sure that the Christian story we tell to children is not a travesty of the original. We need to know who a child is because the enigma of childhood and the mystery of the kingdom of God are not two different secrets. But above all we need to recover a sense of what childhood is for our children's sake, lest they forfeit their childhood too soon.

Frank Kendon (1950) hoped that in uncovering the secrets of childhood he might offer 'a particular addition to the joy of the world'. He wants something more than that we should enjoy his book. Kendon believes that to retrieve our childhood is a benediction—even if memories of childhood are sometimes dark. Here is a final reason for 'wrestling with childhood's angel'. I seek a distinct and specific blessing, an addition, however small, to the sum of human happiness. This essay will not evade the plight of childhood or the threat to childhood, but my hope is that it will bring more joy than sadness, however small that happy increment might be.

CHAPTER 2

'The corn was orient and immortal wheat'

Thaumasia

'The corn was orient and immortal wheat, which never should be reaped, nor was ever sown. I thought it had stood from everlasting to everlasting' (Thomas Traherne, *Centuries*, 110).

Thomas Traherne's lyrical word-picture of what a cornfield looked like to him as a little child is often quoted. We relish the radiant language. But what matters about this description is not its eloquence but its accuracy. It is a correct description. Adults who do not notice that corn is 'orient and immortal wheat' fail to see what they are looking at. We shall see in this chapter that the capacity to notice is an essential aspect of the spirituality of childhood.

Harold Edward (Hal) Porter was an Australian novelist, playwright, poet, and short-story writer. His remarkable memoir *The Watcher on the Cast-Iron Balcony* (Porter, 1963) is an act of recollection, rarely matched in our literature, of the nature, range, detail, and intensity of the child's sensory responses. Porter notes, for example, 'the untainted animal hearing' of the very small child. Alas, it is a fleeting capacity.

'Very little later, the ability to distinguish without hesitation or mistake whether, for example, Mother, unseen in the next room, is talking while lying down or talking while standing or talking while moving about or talking while sitting and brushing her hair, is an ability I lose' (Porter, 1963, 15).

The title of Porter's memoir is significant. The child he once was spent much of his waking hours simply observing, registering all his senses imparted. So do most children, even if perhaps few children recollect what their senses told them as well as Hal Porter. As we grow older and our minds distract us from those primary sense impressions, most of us suffer a decline in our capacity to notice. It is a failure of the spirit as well as of the senses.

To capture the character of objects seen in their true light, as children see them, I borrow a word that occurs just once in the Greek New Testament. *Thaumasia* means 'wonderful things'. *Thaumasia* is the word the gospel-writer Matthew uses to describe the wonders Jesus does in the temple after his entry into Jerusalem. Jesus not only drives out the traders and money-changers; he also heals the blind and the lame. Matthew tells us that the temple authorities were angry when they saw what Jesus was doing. They were still angrier when they noticed the children there, children who—only making matters worse—were cheering him. But for Jesus it is the children alone who see the significance of the *thaumasia*, the wonderful things, he is doing. Jesus reminds the Dean and Chapter of the temple of what the Psalmist said, 'Out of the mouths of infants and nursing babies you have prepared praise for yourself' (Matthew 21.14-16).

Children are surrounded by *thaumasia*. These 'wonderful things' are not necessarily spectacular events such as sunsets, firework displays—or miracles. Nor are they confined to special places like temples.

Serghei Aksakoff grew up in a household furnished with valuables far too costly to be found in the homes of the peasantry on his family's estates. But his own *thaumasia* were simpler. 'To me even the water running down the streets was a joy' (Aksakoff, 1923, 43-44). Serghei's father shows his little son round the local mill and, together, they watch it at work. The child notices everything, the great water-wheel turning slowly, the grain falling through the wooden hopper, the mighty millstones. 'The thought of these marvels,' he writes—and we notice that 'marvels' is the word he uses—'kept me long in a state of astonishment' (Aksakoff, 1923, 45). (Bertram Smith, growing up in the Scottish Highlands, shared the child Aksakoff's delight: 'Of all the legitimate playthings there was none in more constant favour than running water' (Smith, 1920, 33)).

Here is a child who finds wonder in things that to the adult, who has lost the child's eye view, are familiar and commonplace.

Thomas Traherne deplores trying to dazzle children or to win their affection with spectacular presents—'tinselled ware upon a hobby horse', he calls them. He drily recalls how unimpressed he was by the extravagant gifts grown-ups gave him. 'They did impose upon me, and intrude their gifts that made me believe a ribbon or a feather curious. I could not see where was the curiousness or the fineness' (Traherne, 1960, 114).

Bridget Blake remembers Christmas on the Falkland Islands in the early years of the last century. The presents the children exchanged were necessarily simple, but they were *thaumasia* none the less.

> 'There were no shops in which to buy presents, so, if we were going to give anything we had to make or find it. Once my big brother made me a little boat and gave it me floating in a tinfull of water; that was a lovely present. Another time, I had two bits of candle-end, picked up by my sister on the beach. One of the most successful presents ever given was a large cotton reel at the end of a piece of string; my little brother danced all round the room with it singing, "Doodly-doodly-doo-te-doo"' (Blake, 2002, chapter 9).

The poet James Kirkup had unusual powers of recall, remembering even his infancy in sharp detail. He recalls that his early childhood was a world furnished with *thaumasia*, though the things he found wonderful might not have seemed so to adult eyes. In his first volume of autobiography *The Only Child*, which closes with his sixth birthday, Kirkup remembers such marvels as the boot-scraper by the front-door of the family home and the treasures hidden behind it, 'a matchstick, a piece of gravel, a pink tram-ticket, a button' (Kirkup, 1957, 20).

Bryan Magee, brought up in London's East End before its slums were cleared, a neighbourhood few adults would have described in glowing terms, remembers his sense as a child of 'the marvellousness and extraordinariness of everything'.

> 'To the eye and mind of someone in the condition I am speaking of everything seems wonderful, the world an amazing place, disclosing miracles at every turn, and all imparting a kind of ecstatic pleasure' (Magee, 2003, 185-186).

We note his choice of words. The world disclosed '*miracles* at every turn'. Some will say that if everything is marvellous and extraordinary, then nothing is marvellous and extraordinary. If all is miracle, nothing is miracle. But the argument is both fallacious and forgetful. It is just as fallacious as the assertion that if everything is good then nothing is good. It is forgetful too, the conclusion of a mind that no longer recalls how once the world looked.

Spirited Senses

Thaumasia are wonders of the child's first world, perceived by the senses. Very soon all manner of wonders—and terrors too—will arise from within, springing from the fertile ground of the child's imagination. There will be more to say later about all that was magical and menacing about that inner world of childhood. Here we register what comes first, those primal responses, experiences beginning, some would claim, even before the child is born. The testimony of our memoirs is that there is a spiritual dimension to these early sensory experiences, especially to the perceptions—fragmentary as memories of them often are—of the first few years of childhood.

Adults distinguish between the sensory—the sensual too—and the spiritual. Indeed that distinction is already being made in the middle years of childhood and in adolescence. It is a misleading distinction, a misunderstanding begetting, for example, absurd misreadings of the biblical *Song of Songs*, and little children do not make it. With calamitous consequences, Western thought has been dominated by a dualism that opposes the physical and the spiritual. For the youngest children, untroubled by this dualist worldview, body and soul are one.

The writer and psychotherapist Elisaveta Fen was born and brought up in Russia in the early years of the twentieth century. Later she became a British subject. As a little girl she learned to dance. Dancing for her was a single rapturous experience of both body and spirit. 'This was ecstasy, to be compared only with the dreams of flying,' she writes. 'I did not know then that I was on the point of discovering how a state of the body could become a means for attaining the exaltation of the spirit' (Fen, 1961,

247). Of course the distinction Elisaveta Fen makes here between the means and the end, between the physical and the spiritual, is her adult retrospective analysis. The child she was made no such distinction.

When the Pulitzer prize-winning author Annie Dillard was a little girl, she was fascinated by adults' skin. 'They were loose in their skins all over, except at the wrists and ankles, like rabbits.' Her mother lets her play with one of her hands.

> 'I picked up a transverse pinch of skin over the knuckle of her index finger and let it drop. The pinch didn't snap back; it lay dead across her knuckle in a yellowish ridge. I poked it; it slid over intact. I left it there as an experiment and shifted to another finger.'

She notices the hair on her father's arms and legs. 'I lifted a hair and studied the puckered tepee of skin it pulled with it.' She studies her own skin too. 'Skin was earth; it was soil. I could see in my own skin, the joined trapezoids of dust specks God had wetted and stuck with his spit the morning he made Adam from dirt.'

She is pleased with her own skin and with her physical condition generally. Grown-ups, by contrast, were 'coming apart'. (That said, she grants that adults, despite their appalling decrepitude, sometimes do look magnificent and it is they who own the world.) The spiritual, the child's intuitive awareness of the order of things, cannot be separated from the sensory. The sense of how things are is one with the sensation of touching old skin (Dillard, 1987, 24-27).

Sight and sound, touch and taste, and not least smell, are 'spirited senses', the senses that enable children to recognise the wonder of the things that furnish their world and the mystery of those that populate it—a recognition that dawns long before it can be verbalised.

Annie Dillard writes, 'A young child knows Mother as a smelled skin' (35). Our spirituality is our capacity to know the other, our *relational* awareness' as Nye and Hay have taught us to understand it. That awareness is sensory long before it is conceptual. Children know long before they know they know. So by spirited senses, by taste and touch and smell, the child relates to its mother. Only much later will the mind add its assent.

'A young child knows Mother as a smelled skin.' It is worth staying for some time with those *smells* recalled from childhood, both because our writers so often speak of them and commentators on children's spirituality never do. (I suspect that 'the spirituality of smell' is a field I have to myself.)

The children's writer Rosemary Sutcliffe remembers how what she smelled became the vehicle of 'somewhere else' and 'something more'. She recalls her life as a child in a 'little bungalow lost in the pinewoods above Headley Down'. (Headley Down is a village in Hampshire in the south of England).

> 'My memories of Headley Down are strung together on smells. The smell of leaf-mould and pine woods and bonfire smoke and frost; and above all of lamp smitch...Even now, the smell of lamp smitch, which most people find unpleasant, is to me one of those magic smells which open doorways in the mind, letting out the sights and sounds and other smells of some place and time which might otherwise, little by little, be lost and forgotten' (*Blue Remembered Hills* Sutcliffe, 1984, 47).

'Lamp smitch'—later Rosemary Sutcliffe will use this rare and odd term, referring to the acrid smell of an oil lamp, in her celebrated children's story about the Romans in Britain, *The Eagle of the Ninth* (Oxford University Press, 1984). When she tells us that the smell of lamp smitch is 'one of those magic smells that open doorways', she is no doubt simply making the point that, for the adult, a smell can bring back memories, as other sense impressions can—as, most famously, did the taste of a madeleine for Marcel Proust. But her comments suggest more. They invite us to reflect how sense impressions can 'open doorways' for the child too, operating not so much as reminders, more as means of grace, accessing 'the other and the beyond'.

Nigel Slater is a 'celebrity chef'. His *Toast* is a glorious celebration of all that appealed to—and sometimes repelled—a child's sense of taste. But it is the smells as much as the tastes that he remembers.

> 'Forget scented candles and freshly brewed coffee. Every home should smell of baking Christmas cake. That, and warmed freshly

ironed tea towels hanging on the rail in front of the Aga. It was a pity we had Auntie Fanny living with us. Her incontinence could take the edge of the smell of a chicken curry, let alone a baking cake' (Slater, 2003, 3-4).

The writer Colin Middleton Murry, best known for the science-fiction he wrote under the name Richard Cowper, describes his first impressions of the Old Rectory, Larling, the house to which his family moved when he was five. 'What made the most profound impact on me,' he writes, 'was the immense range of unfamiliar smells. They broke over me like so many waves.'

'Fresh distemper and moist, scrubbed bricks in echoing sculleries and dairies, the intoxicating perfume of clove carnations in the walled garden; fizzing acid in the glass accumulator cells in the battery house; last year's rotted conker leaves; musty, sparrow-riddled reed thatch on the ancient summer-house...'
So begins the long catalogue of rich aromas the boy remembers.
'So firmly did these scents imprint themselves upon my five-year-old memory that I have only to catch a whiff of them today and I am at once transported back to that first dreamlike encounter' (Murry, 1975, 39).

The Indian writer Mulk Raj Anand's *Seven Summers* is one of our most sensuous accounts of childhood. One by one, Anand introduces us to the members of his colourful family and to the fascinating characters he meets about the barracks where his father is stationed. His Aunt Aqqi is his mother's youngest sister. The two sisters are altogether different.

'Not only did they look different, but I noticed, *since that was my first instinctive way of getting to know people*, that they also smelt different. My mother was...milk and sugar, but my aunt Aqqi was like the essence of curds' (Anand, 2005, 13).

The words I have italicised draw attention to the importance of the sense of smell in the equipment a very young child deploys to distinguish one person from another. We have no reason to suppose that the way Anand perceived others—'as Aunt Aqqi bent down to kiss me I smelt the acrid smell of her armpits' (14)—was any different from the means by which other children register their encounters with the grown-ups populating their worlds.

Serghei Aksakoff's account of a childhood spent in a Russian patriarchal family, in the closing years of the eighteenth century, is among the most important of our memoirs of childhood. Aksakoff has bequeathed us a towering masterpiece, a work unmatched not only for its detailed description of the everyday life of Russian minor nobility but also for its record of the intense inner life of an exceptionally sensitive child. Aksakoff recalls the smells of his nursery.

> 'I was very fond of the smell of resin, which was sometimes used to fumigate our nursery. I smelt the sweet transparent blobs of resin, admired them, and played with them; they melted in my hands and my made my long thin fingers sticky' (Aksakoff, 1923, 4).

James Kirkup, who remembered the boot-scraper by his front door, also remembers lying in his pram. What he especially recalls is the pram's smell.

> 'There were the mingled aromas of warm leather and oilcloth, a faint hint of wee-wee, and the fragrance of a frilled linen pillow-slip' (Kirkup, 1957, 21).

Bryan Magee liked to linger in the local chandler's, where you went for whatever your horse needed. He used to wander between the huge standing sacks of barley and oats.

> 'When I thrust my face over one—or better still into it, like a nosebag—it made me swoon with the aroma, not shallow like other smells but a deep, solid smell, a smell you could almost sink your teeth into' (Magee, 2003, 36).

The philosopher Richard Wollheim's childhood was far grander than Bryan Magee's, but for him too it is the smells that stay with him, among them the smell of the metal-polish and toothpaste used by the family chauffeur, the smell of mothballs, and the smell of church (Wollheim, 2004, 33, 43, 66).

The poet—and (for the English), national treasure—the late John Betjeman devotes much of his wonderful verse autobiography *Summoned by Bells* to the world of his childhood. It was, above all, a world rich in smells. Betjeman introduces his celebration of those smells with a shout -'Nose! Smell again the early morning smells: Congealing bacon and my father's pipe'. Alas, the recital of these ripe aromas that assailed him extends over too many lines to repeat here. (Betjeman, 1960, 38-39).

We could easily multiply from our memoirs yet more examples of the smells of childhood, pervasive and penetrating, that linger in the memory. (Bea Howe, who grew up in Valpariso's large English community at the end of the Victorian era, bids for a late mention. Little Bea, solemn and shy and painfully unable to express her feelings, adored her dazzling mother, but refused to kiss her because of the smell of her smoking (Howe, *A Child in Chile*, Howe, 37).)

I dwell on such memories—to reiterate—because our writers so frequently do so.

We wonder why those intense smells should have been so important to the child, even somehow significant, as the adult now recognises they were. Walter Benjamin is one of the few writers to address the question. His autobiographical masterpiece *Berlin Childhood around 1900* tells us why, for instance, the smell of a baked apple meant so much to him. Taken from the oven, the apple contained:

'the aromas of all the things the day had in store for me. So it was not surprising that, whenever I warmed my hands on its shining cheeks, I would always hesitate to bite in. I sensed that the fugitive knowledge conveyed by its smell could all too easily escape me on the way to my tongue. That knowledge was so heartening that it stayed to comfort me on my trek to school' (Benjamin, 2006, cited in *The Guardian Review*, 9ᵗʰ August 2014).

The smell of the apple conveys fugitive but comforting knowledge. Reflecting on Benjamin's careful and precise choice of words, we can suggest that, for this little boy, the sensory proved sacramental. In bringing knowledge and comfort what is sensed—in the manner of all sacraments— effects what it signifies. Neither Walter Benjamin the adult, nor, still less, Walter Benjamin the child, can fully explain all that that fragrant baked apple means, but such is ever the mystery of the sacramental.

Richard Wollheim—as we saw a moment ago—remembered 'the smell of church', a recollection that beckons us down an important byway. Many smells linger in churches.

James Joyce's celebrated account of his boyhood is rich in memorable aromas, including that of the chapel of his Jesuit boarding school.

'There was a cold night smell in the chapel. But it was a holy smell. It was not like the smell of the old peasants who knelt at the back of chapel at Sunday mass. That was a smell of air and rain and turf and corduroy' (Joyce, 1992, 18).

Children will certainly be aware of the 'holy smell' of church, but incense, should it be deployed, will not be the only smell they register. Alison Utley, a prolific writer best known for her children's series about 'Little Grey Rabbit' and 'Sam Pig', grew up at the turn of the twentieth century on a remote hill-top farm in Derbyshire. She is the 'Susan' of her semi-fictional account of her childhood. As a child she routinely went to church. Church-going was primarily an assault on her senses. She tells us that 'some wonderful smell on a lady's dress disturbed her.' She reaches for the ivory handle of her mother's umbrella. 'Susan rubbed it with one finger and softly rubbed it against her cheek'—and then her mind wanders to Africa, 'with its green parrots, crocodiles, tigers...(and) elephants pounding through the jungle on legs like beech trunks'. She studies the gentry in church. 'She wondered why they had such big noses and thick hair. She listened to the swish, swish of their skirts as they walked in front of her up the aisle and she sniffed at the lovely smells coming from their clothes' (Utley, 1936, 33-41).

Most children no longer go to church, but it is certain that those who still do will be as alert as Susan was to the smell and the feel, to the sights and the sounds, of the place. Not least to the smell.

The earliest memories of religion are of what the senses register. John Gross, the son of a Jewish doctor who practised in the East End of London before the Second World War and a former editor of the *Times Literary Supplement*, recalls the family dinner table on Friday night, the eve of the Sabbath. He remembers 'watching the melted wax trickle down the side of a candlestick and harden into a blob (so satisfying to peel away afterwards)'. Nothing stands out more clearly for him in his memory of the beginning of Passover than 'the almost inevitable spillage of red wine on a fresh white tablecloth...and the darker red stains left by fragments of *chrein*, horseradish sauce laced with beetroot' (Gross, 2001, 15-16).

Andrew Motion, who will one day become the Poet Laureate, describes his first night away from home at his prep school. In his dormitory he puts the Bible his mother has given him under his pillow. 'I squeezed it,' he tells us, 'and the leather felt like a hand under my pillow. I'd do that every night, I decided...Maybe God would travel up my arm and get into my brain and help me with my work'. It is not the words of the Bible, not any of its comforting promises, which reassure the child and strengthen him in spirit, but what is physically palpable, the touch of a leather-bound book (Motion, 2006, 105).

We wonder how many more memories of the *feel* of a Bible we might come across had we the time to hunt them down. Paul Ashton grew up in a strict Plymouth Brethren family. He begins his account of his childhood with an extraordinary extended description of what the family Bible meant to him as a four-year-old. He tells us how it was too heavy for him to lift and how the ribs on its spine left pale parallel impressions on his thighs. The child is awed by the embossed gold Gothic letters on the Bible's cover. 'I was half thrilled by the book's weight and splendour,' he tells us, 'and half frightened by my own powerlessness and vulnerability compared to it'. The little boy delights in lifting a single page of this wonderful book. 'While I held it, it was proud to be noticed by me, I could tell, but when I let it fall back it gave up its individuality willingly...I thought how very happy it must be.'

Long before he can read it, this book is already a *thaumasion*, a marvel, a thing of wonder. 'I wondered who could conceive, design, make, bind and deliver to us such a thing.' And, needless to say, there are the rich smells of this glorious object. 'My nose was very close to the book, and took in the mixed smells of leather, brass, and paper as it was opened.' Ashton adds, 'I have been caught more than once since then, sniffing at Bibles on lecterns in country churches, trying to recapture the smell' (Ashton, 2011, 9-11).

Religion is a troubling realm to which we shall return. Meanwhile we would do well to ponder the happy fact that the verb 'to feel' means two things among more. The child who feels a mother's kiss feels a mother's love. The experience is sacramental—the sensory and the spiritual are one.

'All appeared new and strange at first'

The young child's experience is of the specific and timeless. When our writers search their earliest memories it is the distinct and sharply focussed detail which comes back to them. As Bryan Magee recalls:

'When I was small...my face was so near the ground that I saw in vivid close-up everything that was under my nose. I knew each paving-stone in the street immediately outside where we lived, each with its own actual shape and colour' (Magee, 2003, 4).

The poet, Kathleen Raine recollects how the objects of her Northumberland childhood existed as specific timeless presences, for example 'a little hand of flame, blue-tipped, thin, labile, without substance or constant form, dancing gently on a gas-jet from the wall'. She lived, she tells us, 'in a world of flowers'. 'Each and every one greeted me *in a here and now that had no beginning and no end*' (Raine, 1973, 12-13). My italics are to underscore the immediacy of the child's awareness.

Children see as for the first time. Elisaveta Fen, who grew up in Russia in the early years of the twentieth century, observes, 'One characteristic of my earliest memories is their very narrow field, limited perhaps by my complete absorption in whatever was happening to me at that moment' (Fen, 1961, 14). For Emma Smith, author of one of our memorable Cornish memoirs, everything was new. She remembers her 'first world', the world in which 'every scarlet pillar box, every gate and bush and tree and flower, was new and equally fascinating' (Smith, 2008, 4-5). It is this sheer novelty of things, as the child perceives them, that is so marvellously captured by Thomas Traherne. Traherne remembers how 'all appeared new and strange at first, inexpressibly rare and delightful and beautiful' (Traherne, 1960, 109). Children, at least in their infancy, see by 'the first Light', by 'the same light and in the same colours' as Adam saw in Paradise (113).

The naturalist Richard Jefferies records how Bevis, the boy who Jefferies himself once was, and his friend Mark listen to the singing of a waterfall. The flowers and trees attend too. The glorious passage warrants quoting at length:

> 'The forget-me-nots and the hart's tongue, the beeches and the firs listened to the singing. Something had gone by, and something that was to come, came out of the music and made this moment sweeter. This moment of the singing held a thousand years that had gone by, and the thousand years that are to come. For the woods and the waters are very old: that is the past; if you look up into the sky you know that a thousand years hence will be nothing to it: that is the future. But the forget-me-nots and the hart's tongue, and the beeches did not think of the ages gone, or the azure to come. They were there now, the sunshine and the wind above, the shadow and the water and the spray beneath—that was all in all. Bevis and Mark were there now, listening to the singing, that was all in all.'

'"There never was a yesterday," whispered the wind to Bevis, "and there will never be tomorrow. It is all one long today"' (Jefferies, 1881, 377).

Frederick Buechner, one of America's finest religious writers, directs us to Dylan Thomas's poem *Fern Hill*.

> 'And once below a time I lordly had the trees and leaves
> Trail with daisies and barley
> Down the rivers of the windfall light.'

Buechner takes it that 'once below a time' means,

> 'that for a child, time in the sense of something to measure and keep

track of, time as the great circus parade of past, present, and future, cause and effect, has scarcely started yet and means little because for a child all time is by and large now time and apparently endless' (Buechner, 1982, 9).

We shall have occasion to return later to *Fern Hill*—rightly acclaimed as one of the loveliest evocations of childhood in the English language.

Then and now

The Russian novelist Konstantin Paustovsky remembers his childhood at the end of the nineteenth century.

'In childhood, everything was different. Everything was more vivid—the sun brighter, the smell of the field sharper, the thunder louder, the grain more abundant and the grass taller. And our hearts were bigger, our griefs more poignant, and our country—that soil of our birth which is the greatest gift we have in life, to tend, care for and protect with our whole being—was more enigmatic' (Paustovsky, 1964, 84-85).

The comparatives—'brighter', 'sharper', 'louder' and the rest—are the adult's. They reflect the grown-up's recognition of failing senses, of glory yielding to the light of common day. Children, living in 'the continuous now' of their young lives, do not make such comparisons. For them, things are neither better nor worse. They are as they are. Only adults contrast how things once seemed with how they appear today. But our mature ability to make such comparisons does not mean that we perceive more accurately. To have seen it all before does not mean to see more truly.

Some fear that little can be done about this loss. The Danish composer Carl Nielsen bewails the damage we do to children as they grow up. He feels that that damage is beyond repair. We rob our children, he suggests, of a vision of life which is essentially poetic.

'Poetic talent, I imagine, is fundamentally the faculty, the gift, of distinctive observation and perception. Thus we have at all at one time been poets and artists, each after his manner. The rough way in which life and adults summon the child from its beautiful world of poetry and art to harsh matter-of-fact reality must, I think, be blamed for the fact that most of us forfeit these talents, with the result that the divine gift of imagination, innate in the child, becomes mere day-dreaming or is quite lost' (Nielsen, 1953, 9).

The primal loss, Nielsen claims, is the capacity to notice.

Other writers, perhaps those who have made a better fist of growing-up, do not mourn the loss of the child's eye view but reflect more positively on how the way we saw things as children shapes our adult perceptions.

Eleanor Acland, prominent member of the women's suffrage movement, grew up in a grand house on a great estate in Devonshire. She suggests that if we still delight in certain sights—'snowdrops on dark patches of grass among just melting snow', for example—it is because they preserve something of the intense impact they made on us when we saw them as children for the first time (Acland, 1935, 23).

Herbert Read agrees. *The Innocent Eye*, the first part of his *Annals of Innocence and Experience*, records the beginning of an extraordinary journey, the path that will take him from his boyhood on a remote farm in the Yorkshire Dales to his eminence as one of the foremost poets and critics of the twentieth century. Read suggests that our only real experiences are our first experiences, 'those lived with a virgin sensibility'. Later experiences are, at best, only echoes.

'We only hear a tone once, only see a colour once, see, hear, touch, taste, and smell everything but once, the first time. All life is an echo of our first sensations, and we build up our consciousness, our whole mental life, by variations and combinations of these elementary sensations' (Read, 1946, 19).

The young child's 'spirited senses' shape the sensibilities of the adult. 'The seclusion of my first ten years,' he writes, 'now seems like an age of unearthly bliss, a ring in a rock to which all the strands of my subsequent happiness are tied' (67). For Read, as for Wordsworth, 'the child is father of the man'. Read's reflections recapitulate the argument of Wordworth's *Immortality Ode,* that 'in our embers is something that doth live.' The realm of childhood is never wholly lost. 'The bright points of ecstasy that enlighten our later days,' Read claims, 'come from the heart of this lost realm'.

Read describes shelling the pods of a withered stem of the plant honesty between his thumb and finger. The sensations he experiences as he does the same as an adult 'come direct to me from a moment thirty years ago'. The recollection of that first seminal experience—we might say of that first 'spirited touch'—triggers a widening circle of other primal memories.

> 'The low box-hedge which would be at my feet, the pear trees on the wall behind me, the potato flowers on the patch behind the bushes...Everything shimmers for a second on the expanding rim of my memory.'

Read concludes,

> 'The farthest tremor of this perturbation is lost only at the finest edge where sensation passes beyond the confines of experience; for memory is a flower which only opens fully in the kingdom of Heaven, where the eye is eternally innocent' (Read, 1946, 60-61).

The sacrament of the present moment

'Memory is a flower which only opens fully in the kingdom of Heaven.' We hear behind Herbert Read's allusive words Jesus's warning that unless we become like children we shall not enter God's kingdom (Matthew 18.3). That warning is our mandate for asking what we may learn from the child Herbert Read was, and from the other children we are meeting, about the disciples we must become.

There is a chorus that used to be taught to Sunday school children:

> '*Turn your eyes upon Jesus,*

Look full in his wonderful face,
And the things of earth will grow strangely dim
In the light of his glory and grace.'

The song asks the impossible of the child, to separate the spiritual and the sensory. Mystics will claim that there are levels of spiritual experience that rise above the physical and material. But we are not required to become mystics—at least not just yet. We are required to become children. If I turn and become as a child, the things of earth—earth's *thaumasia*—will not grow strangely dim. On the contrary, they will become strangely bright.

It follows that Christian discipleship requires renewed attention to what we rarely notice, 'the things of earth'—the literally mundane—about which the children's chorus is so dismissive. Does that mean that, as little James Kirkup did, we should pay attention to matchsticks, buttons, and the rest? Three considerations suggest that such consideration of trifles may not be entirely whimsical or absurd. First, we rarely pay attention to the commonplace and we ought not to scorn what we have never tried. Secondly, if obedience to the word of Jesus about becoming a child means behaving apparently foolishly then so does most of his moral teaching. Thirdly—and above all—Christianity is a faith that affirms the material. Matter matters. In a word that we have found ourselves using more than once in this chapter, Christianity is a *sacramental* faith. The ordinary—a fragment of bread, a sip of wine—can be a means of grace.

Christian faith and worship are grounded in the principle that the sensory can be charged with the spiritual. This we know by what douses us at our baptism and by what we taste at the Eucharist. Material things can be more than they materially are. The Chilean poet Pablo Neruda, though not a Christian believer, filled his several houses with *things*, old bottles, hammers, seashells, compasses, and all manner of other objects. In a word, he collected *thaumasia*. This he did because he remained at heart a child for whom nothing was merely ordinary.

'Christians must learn to wonder before they can reign or rest.' The maxim, from a papyrus fragment found on an ancient rubbish dump in Egypt, is the truth our memoirs are telling us. In some Christian churches much is made of 'baptism of the spirit'. Nothing less is required of us than a baptism of the senses.

Also required of us is a renewed sense of time, a reawakened awareness of the irrecoverable present. Philip Simmons, living with a terminal degenerative illness, wrote in his moving volume of essays *Learning to Fall,*

'The present moment, like the spotted owl or the sea turtle, has become an endangered species. Yet more and more I find that dwelling in the present moment, in the face of everything that would call us out of it, is our highest spiritual discipline. More boldly, I would say that our very presentness is our salvation; the present moment, entered into fully, is our gateway to eternal life' (Simmons, 2000, 145).

Simmons echoes the French Jesuit Jean Pierre de Caussade (1675-1871) who famously wrote of the 'the sacrament of the present moment' (de Caussade, 1921). The children we meet in our memoirs receive that sacrament, live in that moment. It is not easy for adults, dogged by the past, fearful of the future, to dwell in the present. But the word of Jesus, calling us to become as children, requires us to do our best to do so, to recognise each instant as a gift from God.

The here, the now—and the not yet

For children, the sensory and the spiritual are inseparable. Now is where children live. These characteristics of the growing child have far-reaching implications for the child's learning. One example of an approach to Christian nurture which recognises the role of the sensory in a child's appreciation of the Christian story and in the acquisition of Christian language is that developed over many years by Jerome Berryman and known as 'Godly Play'. In a Godly Play lesson the story unfolds by the use of artefacts. Often the lesson will begin with the opening of a golden box, the box containing the figures and the fabrics that will feature in the story for the day. These artefacts do not merely illustrate the story; they bear the weight of the story as much as do the teacher's words. The teacher is respectful of the palpable 'there-ness' of the artefacts he is using, as the children will be too. They are the centre of attention for teacher and children alike. 'Look at me and then I'll know that you're listening!' is not a rubric used in Godly Play.

Later in the lesson the children will have the opportunity to handle these artefacts themselves or others they choose from the range of materials on shelves around the Godly Play classroom. These artefacts are simple, but they are made with love. During the lesson they are handled slowly and with deliberation, just as the words the teacher uses are sparing and carefully chosen. These things are *thaumasia*.

The pedagogical roots of Godly Play in the work of Maria Montessori and Sofia Cavalletti are manifest, but the theological roots are deeper still. We recall the text that Frank Kendon chose as an epigraph to *The Small Years*.

'That which from the beginning, which we have heard, which we have seen with our eyes, which we have looked upon, and our hands have handled of the word of life' (1 John 1.1).

'That which our hands have handled'. In its use of materials which a child's hands can handle, Godly Play recognises both the primal importance of the sensory in a child's learning and the sacramental principle that 'matter matters', that 'mere things' can be means of grace. In the context of the church these 'mere things' may well be the playthings a teacher provides. There are all those treasures beckoning from the shelves of the Godly Play classroom. Certainly if we fail to provide children with things to play with the sensory deprivation they will surely suffer will be a spiritual deprivation too. But if we have learned one truth from this chapter it is that the marvellous things that children find for themselves, as much as those pressed on them by adults, can be sacramental too.

Whether or not we use Godly Play in teaching our children, the truth about children, which that approach reflects and our memoirs show, must underpin the methods we use. Not least we should give far more thought to what our classrooms smell like.

Historically the church's word to children, at least in the West, has been 'not yet'. The grounds of this pronouncement have been theologies, for there have been numerous, spun by adults for adults, which disregard children entirely. Because these theologies have no room for children, the latter have been left in a kind of limbo. (Limbo, we recall, was the melancholy realm, neither heaven nor hell, which was held to be the destination of infants dying before they were baptised.) In the western catholic tradition, 'not yet' is said to children who are refused the sacrament of Holy Communion until they satisfy the conditions which the church says they must meet. In the evangelical tradition children are 'outside'—old enough to go to hell, too young to go to heaven—until they 'decide for Christ'. Both schools of theological thought, the catholic and the evangelical, have gone far in recent years to ameliorate the status of the child in the church, but the legacy of the old attitudes remains.

This is not the place to refute theologies that prevaricate about the status of children in the church, a status about which, were he allowed any say in the matter, Jesus of Nazareth is wholly unequivocal. That work has been done elsewhere, nowhere more powerfully and eloquently than in Horace Bushnell's *Christian Nurture*, first published in 1847. Here I simply underline what emerges so clearly from our memoirs. The young child lives in the here and the now. If as a young child I am given to understand that I am not yet fully one of the Christian family, then, however much I am entertained in church by kindly and well-meaning people, I will know in my heart that I am not really wanted.

CHAPTER 3

OTHER WORLDS—UNSEEN FRIENDS

The things that to the adult seem unremarkable can be the source of wonder to a little child. These *thaumasia*—the pebble on the shore, the snail on the leaf, the bits and pieces ending up behind a boot-scraper—are at least tangibly part of our world. But for children there are other worlds too, realms just as real as the world our five senses make known to us. In these other worlds too there are wonders to enjoy and friends to be made.

The Irish novelist William Trevor reminds us that children—at least as they emerge from infancy—lead a double life. For Trevor there was on the one hand 'the ordinariness of dressing in the morning, putting on shoes and combing hair, stirring a spoon through porridge I did not want, and going at ten to nine to the nun's elementary school.' But there was also 'a world in which only the events I wished for happened, where boredom was not permitted and of which I was both God and King' (Trevor, 1997, 19). (Though no doubt there will have been a time when, for a yet younger William Trevor, the ritual of getting up and getting dressed would not have been so 'ordinary', but rather an adventure renewed every morning.)

'Everything that can be imagined is real,' said Pablo Picasso. How much of this other world is indeed *there*—there as much as the low beam on which you bang your head—and how much is mere make-believe is a philosophical and theological issue beyond the remit of this study to discuss. But a marker needs to be put down. We do not exclude the possibility that there is an existent order answering to what the child imagines. If there is indeed such a place, it is certainly better than the worlds some of our children grew up in.

The spirituality of slum childhoods

Frank McCourt's Pulitzer Prize-winning memoir *Angela's Ashes* has established itself as a classic account of impoverished Irish childhood. We search this extraordinary testimony for indications of how a child survives spiritually in conditions of such extreme deprivation. That search is not fruitless. When Frank's brother Michael was born, his father told Frank that 'he found (Michael) on the seventh step of the stairs to Italy'. ('Italy' is the name the family gave to the upstairs room of their tenement apartment.) His father explains: 'That's what you have to watch out for when you ask for a new baby, "the Angel of the Seventh Step"' (McCourt, 1997, 111). The 'seventh step' becomes sacred to Frank and he sometimes sits there, because that is where the angel is to be met. Later, as the family's miseries multiply, he will conclude that the Angel on the Seventh Step has gone 'some place else' (237).

Here is a child growing up in an almost unimaginably wretched situation. Yet, however forlornly, he still reaches out to a better world beyond. Here is a child becoming aware of the disparity between what life is and what—beyond his ability yet to understand or articulate—life is meant to be.

Growing up in a classic slum is the subtitle of Richard Roberts's account of his Salford childhood. Home is above and behind the family's little corner shop, maintained by the resilience and intelligence of the child's mother. His father is 'fonder of the bottle than the business'. Again the question arises—how can the spiritual thrive when daily life is a continuing struggle to survive? For the child too is caught up in that struggle and soon becomes its victim. It is unsurprising if indicators of the spiritual are sparse when pressing material demands are so relentless. 'The other and the beyond' is hard to experience when the realities of the here and now are harsh and inescapable. (More of this must be said when in our next chapter we come to discuss 'spiritual distress' in childhood.)

But as for Frank McCourt so for Richard Roberts, there are hints of 'the other and the beyond'. There is a spiritual dimension to life spent even in such bleak conditions. In one passage Roberts describes how the small boy he was sometimes wandered out alone into the dark. He hears the ships on the canal blowing their horns—'always for me they were bidding adieu, leaving our squalor and dark vacancy behind and speeding away west to sunlit oceans and some fair Hesperides' (Roberts, 1976, 119-120).

Even in a slum, a child may dream of 'some fair Hesperides'.

Many of our memoirs recall growing up in what we might think were rural idylls. But it is not only in such green and pleasant lands that we find indicators of the spirituality of childhood. At the risk of labouring the point, I turn to two more 'slum childhoods' for evidence.

Helen Forrester, child of a Liverpool slum, longing for education, enrols for an evening class. But she is too poor to buy the books she needs. She breaks down and all her pent-up pain pours out.

'I cried hopelessly and helplessly until not another tear would come...I cried because I was drifting helplessly on a sea of life for which I had not been prepared and which I did not understand. I cried for the perfect peace and safe refuge of my grandmother's house by the sea. I cried because I could not cross the Mersey to reach the green field and wild seashores I loved' (Forrester, 1974, 275).

In this deeply moving memoir 'crossing the Mersey' becomes a metaphor for more than escape from material destitution. It serves as an image of our longing for 'something more', though for what we do not know, the discontent that—as we shall see—some would claim is the surest proof that we are spiritual beings.

Ralph Glasser grew up on the top floor of a tenement in the Gorbals, Glasgow's notorious slums now long demolished. 'At night,' he remembers, 'when everyone was asleep, I often crept to the window and stared out and saw visions'.

'To the east and north on clear nights I could see the stars hanging like distant snowflakes on a vast curtain of dark blue velvet stretched across the world, and I imagined that I pushed my way through the window and stood on the ledge outside and floated away into the sky and journeyed through it deeper and deeper, through limitless space and time'.

The child wrestles with the question of how to encompass the mystery of the heavens. He tells us that one day, when he was about seven, he woke up knowing that he had found 'something apocalyptic'. It was the realisation that if he travelled to the end of the universe and came to a wall, there must be something beyond it. Moreover, if he climbed that wall and travelled on until he came to another wall, still he would have to ask what was on its other side. The child concludes that here was a proof of infinity and, thus, of the existence of God. (Long before, the child Thomas Traherne had speculated about the bounds of the universe. 'My thoughts would be deeply engaged with enquiries: How did the Earth end? Whether walls did bound it, or sudden precipices?' (Traherne, 1960, 118))

Ralph Glasser tries to talk about these things to his sister and his father, but they pooh-pooh his thoughts as too complicated for a small boy.

'All I wanted was someone to see what I had seen. The symmetry I had found was joy in itself. The music of the spheres rang in my head. Alas, such visions, fitting in to no language, a poetry of the soundless ether, I could communicate to no one' (Glasser, 1986, 26-28).

It is a pattern endlessly repeated. Children are unable to make others see what they have seen. For fear that it will be derided or dismissed, they keep the vision to themselves. The consequence can be tragic. The vision, long suppressed, can finally fade and the child, who saw so much further, settles as an adult for the partial account of things that the generality of grown-ups fancy is all to be said about them.

Frank McCourt, Richard Roberts, Helen Forrester, Ralph Glasser— all are children old enough to sense that there is something amiss in the condition of life they experience and to hold out for something better. At one level they simply want things to be different. But there is more to their longing. In a word—though not a word they would have used—they reach for *transcendent*.

This world and another

Kevin Crossley-Holland's childhood in the Chilterns and on holiday on the Norfolk coast was far removed from the slums. We shall come back later to children growing up in the countryside and we shall see how for them nature can be suffused by the spiritual. Here we notice how young Kevin's world merges with another.

'I never doubted for one moment that there were lives and forces and presences around me: fairyfolk and wodwos in the beechwoods; the black dog Shuck, large as a donkey, roaming along the Norfolk saltmarshes where my grandparents lived; ghosts in the churchyard... That I would seldom or never see them made them no less real' (Crossley-Holland, 2009, 10).

This sense of unseen 'lives and forces and presences' surrounding us is pronounced in the Belfast writer Forrest Reid's work. His strange novels, restricted in range but strangely beautiful in their minor key, are all variations on a single theme. The central figure is the child (always a boy) who moves easily between this world and another. That other world is a 'dream-world', but as real to the protagonists of Reid's fiction as the world of their ordinary experience. Reid's stories are manifestos for his belief that our human condition is that of exiles longing to return to their true home. This nostalgia for the paradise from which we are excluded, Reid claims, is the ultimate spring of our artistic and spiritual nature. That nostalgia, Reid insists, already shaped who he was as a child. *Apostate*, his account of his Belfast boyhood, tells of a child answering to the beckoning call of a better world (Reid, 1947).

The poet Kathleen Raine is close in spirit to Forrest Reid. The goal of our pilgrimage, she maintains, is 'that state of lost paradise from which we are all exiles, but to which we must make our return journey, as best we may.' She adds: 'The sense of exile in a foreign land, of being of another race and kind from those among whom I have lived, has not weakened to this day, so deeply was it implanted in my infancy' (Raine, 1973, 21).

Raine's densely written memoir *Farewell Happy Fields*, recalling her childhood in a remote Northumberland hamlet, analyses the experience of an acutely introspective and intensely sensitive child. Was she exceptionally sensitive? Was she a child Walter de la mare might have told us about? Or is it simply her powers of recall that are exceptional and her ability as a poet to speak of feelings many have known but few can express? Perhaps there are rather more children like Kathleen Raine than we realise.

A. L. Rowse, like Forrest Reid, remembers the nostalgia he experienced as a boy. In his celebrated *A Cornish Childhood* he recalls, as he went to sleep, hearing men returning from market, singing Moody and Sankey hymns.

'Even then they held an incurable nostalgia for the small boy who heard them mingled with sleep and drowsy warmth, the security of the walls of home. I recognize it well, that nostalgia which has underlain all my experience of life, in one form or another, like the not always explicit burden of a song' (Rowse, 1942, 13).

The note of nostalgia sounds repeatedly in this memoir, a yearning for the world of which Rowse, a troubled and complicated man, can be at times contemptuous and dismissive. 'I now recognise that nostalgia in some form or other has been the underlying emotion, the undertone, of my whole life.' He adds, 'the religious-minded would have their explanation: they might not be far wrong' (8).

Certainly the mood of nostalgia may mislead writers about their childhood. We shall be well-advised, for example, to approach Kenneth Grahame's *The Golden Age* and *Dream Days*, hypnotically enchanting as they are, with a measure of caution. But the testimony of waspish, sceptical Rowse, who believed that history should be evidence-based, is not to be so lightly dismissed. What is striking in the testimony of such writers as Raine, Reid, and Rowse is their claim to have already felt this sense of nostalgia in their childhood.

This last point must be stressed. Nostalgia does not overtake these writers only as adults. Theirs is not Kenneth Grahame's yearning for childhood, a longing born of his distaste for adult life and his inability to cope with it. Even as children they pined for the beyond. It was a longing, so they would claim, for a realm that somehow—and however obscurely— they had always known.

John Masefield, poet laureate, spoke of 'the ecstatic bliss of his earliest childhood'. But all along he knew that there was 'somewhere better'.

'All that I looked upon was beautiful and known by me to be beautiful, but also known by me to be, as it were, only the shadow of something much more beautiful, very , very near, and almost to be reached, where there was nothing but beauty itself in ecstasy, undying inexhaustible (Masefield, 1952, 11).

Walter de la Mare, who himself told such haunting tales of children not altogether at home in this world, wrote of the poets such as John Masefield, who, from their youngest days, felt that they did not really belong where they had found themselves stranded.

'To be a child, these witnesses, gravely declare, is to be an exile, and an exile haunted with vanishing intimations and relics of another life and of a far happier state of being—of a lost Jerusalem to which it is all in vain (by the waters of Babylon) to pine to return' (de la Mare, 1935, 91).

How widely is this nostalgia, this sense of exile, shared by the majority of children? Few children either speak of such nostalgia—not that they would have words for it—or in later life write about it. Perhaps we should see those who claim to have known such longings—longings for they know not what—as altogether exceptional, if not a little weird.

Or perhaps not. Certainly we have here indicators of a dimension to children's spiritual experience that is scarcely acknowledged, let alone discussed, in the now extensive literature on the spiritual life of children. It is a lamentable lacuna.

When they were children, some of our writers lived very close to the frontier between this world and another. Robin Fedden recalls with exquisite delicacy the porous nature of this frontier. Fedden was born in 1908 and brought up in France, so the years of his childhood were those leading up to and including the Great War. But neither war nor the rumours of war trouble his *Chantemesle*, a lyrical evocation of growing-up on the banks of the Seine. Here is a hidden gem of a book, understated, oblique, subtle, but unerringly exact. For Robin and Clotilde, the daughter of a neighbouring family, the edge of the forest that borders Clotilde's home is not only the frontier between the familiar and the unexplored. It is also the threshold to an alternative world where, Fedden writes, 'the laws that imprison us all were in suspense'. There the child has a sense that he is 'other than himself' (Fedden, 1964, 45-47).

Robin and Clotilde find an ancient well in the forest. As they look into it, 'the dividing line between reality and image was lost' (55).

> 'We hardly knew the paths we walked, or whether the things seen in the glades were fact or fancy. The boundaries of the real and the unreal disappeared...We inhabited a stretch of country that bore no resemblance to anything on a map' (61).

For children like Robin and Clotilde the veil between the worlds wears thin in particular places. For other children the veil is lifted at certain seasons. For Francesca Allinson, child of Bloomsbury—or, at least, its fringes—Christmas was the intimation of another world.

> 'That undoubtedly was the way of the supernatural world: things happened suddenly, without preparation; and at Christmas, when the skin of reality wore thin, the strange blood of the other world showed through' (Allinson, 1937, 187).

Eileen Elias, who, she tells us, occasionally played noughts and crosses with God, was a child of London's suburbia. There was a pear tree at the bottom of her garden. This tree was a feature of one of her two 'green places' to which she escaped occasionally. When she climbs the tree she gets a sense of how God must feel, looking down on his creation. When she rejoins her parents, they ask her what she was doing. She is at a loss what to say.

> 'I never did know how to answer. What *had* I been doing? Dreaming over a pond, watching an underwater world? Climbing a tree and being God? Hiding away in a nowhere-land of red raspberries and green gooseberries? Feeling a touch of the sadness of the world among the broken-pots and ashes of dead fires? How could you tell this to the grown-ups? There simply were not words enough; and if there were they wouldn't understand'.

Eileen's other 'green place' was the local park, the nearest she knew to the real country which she longed for. She climbs to the top of the house so she can catch a glimpse through the attic window of the tops of the trees in the park. 'I clung to that beatific vision of trees which might almost, so very nearly, be the country.' When life was 'particularly worrying'—and, as we shall see, Eileen Elias experienced times of acute inward suffering—she draws comfort from that 'little triangle of green', an oasis that promised 'the peace, the beauty, the steadfastness of the country she longed one day to see.'

Eileen's two green places are tokens and promises of another and better world.

'It took a lot of pretending to turn the narrow uphill garden into some country paradise; or the park, within its iron railings, into the wide open spaces for which I longed. Yet sometimes it happened. Without my knowing it, I was transported to the green places where romance dwelled. Magic things can happen when you are a child' (Elias, 1978, 39-45).

The Irish poet Seamus Heaney describes his favourite hiding-place as a child, the refuge from which all appeared differently.

'All children want to crouch in their secret nests. I loved the fork of a beech tree at the head of our lane, the close thicket of a of a boxwood hedge in the front of the house, the soft, collapsing pile of hay in a back corner of the byre; but especially I spent time in the throat of an old willow tree at the end of the farmyard...Once you squeezed in through it, you were at the heart of a different life, looking out on the familiar yard as if it were suddenly behind a pane of strangeness' (Heaney, 1997, 16).

'The other and the beyond', the realm entered in the child's imagination, can be this nearer world transfigured. When Clifford Dyment's father is killed in the First World War, his mother takes him and his sister to Nottingham, where his father's sister ('Auntie George') and his Uncle 'GB' find lodgings for them with a Mr and Mrs Belton.

The odious Mrs Belton is a heartless, uncaring, hypocritical woman. Her sad, kindly, ailing husband, who worked on the railways all his life, has one consuming passion, the lovingly created model trains he has crafted in the sitting room which is his sanctum. Mr Belton befriends the boy and becomes his 'Homer', introducing him to the lore and legends, the history and the heroes, of the railways. The railway provides for the boy an imaginative escape from his miserable existence in this unhappy home and subsequently from the even more wretched time living with Auntie George and Uncle GB. The lore of the railways provides a language in which he can express his longing for a better life and by which he can touch the transcendent

> 'I saw a good deal of the world in this way: New Guinea, Greenland, Samoa, Morocco, the Sandwich Islands, Tenerife, Salonika, Cochin China, Guadeloupe, Mozambique, the Aegean Islands, Tristan da Cunha, Juan Fernandez, the Bermudas, the Moluccas, the Seychelles, the Celebes, Sarawak, Zanzibar. And at any time I wished I could steam away from the world and cruise among the planets' (Dyment, 1962, 204).

The aspiring spirit ascends on the wings of language. To this fundamental principle we must return.

Encouraged by his father, young Kevin Crossley-Holland built up a small museum of treasures he had collected—old coins, fossils, and Iron Age potsherds among them. This museum fulfils much the same role for him as that of the model railway for the young Clifford Dyment. Crossley-Holland writes,

> 'Irrespective of the circumstances in which children grow up, we make for ourselves (and sometimes in the least appetising and improbable places) secret and healing retreats, where actuality and imagination meet and time stands outside the door' (Crossley-Holland, 2009, 103).

The 'secret and healing retreat' can be a museum in a bedroom or a den in the woods, a location which you, the grown-up, can visit too, if the child invites you. But the wholly imaginary retreat can be just as real. The great Bengali philosopher and poet Rabindranath Tagore (1861-1941) frequently returned to his own childhood in his writings. In his *Reminiscences* he tells us that, as a child, he had a young playmate, perhaps one of the servant girls in his huge family home, who claimed to have visited what she called 'the King's Palace'. The child Tagore senses that the palace must be very near. He wonders where it can be, but he never finds it. Wistfully he reflects,

> 'Looking back on childhood's days the thing that recurs most often is the mystery that used to fill both life and world. Something undreamt of was lurking everywhere... It was as if nature held something in her closed hands and was smilingly asking us: "What do you think I have?"' (Tagore, 1917, 20)

Crossley-Holland recalls being 'where actuality and imagination meet'; Tagore senses his proximity to 'something undreamt of'. Such children—as to a degree all children—are, in a word, 'liminal' beings. Their home is on the edge. That borderland is their native territory. They live at the frontier of the seen and the unseen and there, as Tagore recalls in haunting imagery, is where they play.

> 'On the seashore of endless worlds children meet...They build their houses with sand, and they play with empty shells. With withered leaves they weave their boats and smilingly float them on the vast deep. Children have their play on the seashore of the worlds' (Tagore, 1913a, 54).

Perhaps because I live at the seaside, I find this image of the child playing on the shore extraordinarily fascinating and suggestive. The land is where we are on firm ground, where we know where we are, where we are in charge. The sea is what is beyond, what is both beyond our understanding and beyond our control. The sea is wonderful, but it is, at the same time, fearful.

It is at this boundary between land and sea, between *here* where we are safe, and *there* where, most certainly, we are not safe, children play. Children play on the shore, close to the water's edge. We grown-ups move far 'inland', as Wordsworth puts it. We retreat to our deckchairs and newspapers higher up the beach, if not back to our desks and laptops.

Unseen friends

We have been taught by David Hay and Rebecca Nye that children's spirituality is relational (*The Spirit of the Child*). The relationship many children enjoy is with an 'imaginary' companion. Such relationships have recently received careful study by students of children's spirituality. J. Bradley Wigger has written about them, asking what connection there might be 'between an invisible friend and an invisible God' (Wigger, 2011). Kate Adams's *Unseen Worlds* explores how children 'see the unseen' and the importance to them of their 'invisible friends' (Adams, 2010).

We meet many such companions in our memoirs. The writer Paul Bailey's most enjoyable moments were spent in the company of an imagined twin brother. Sometimes, in his imagination, he *becomes* the lively brother he has created for himself. Becoming his imagined twin allows him to escape from a home life in which he is never really sure whether he is truly wanted (Bailey, 1990, 7).

Such companions can be as real and important to the child as those of flesh and blood who visibly people their lives. Imaginary friends need not be other boys and girls. Later we shall meet children who made friends with trees. Susan (Alison Uttley) befriends, and is befriended by, the moon.

> 'Susan walked along with her eyes on the moon's golden face. The path was dim, but she was unafraid, for the crowding trees were asleep, the powers were harmless, and the moon, this spiritual unearthly friend, was her companion' (Uttley, 1936, 139).

> 'She never looked at him through glass when he was new, for he hated mirrors and windows until he was full-grown, and she always bowed to him, as her mother had taught her' (142). The moon 'fetches Susan out of bed' one night. She goes down to kitchen and lets herself out of the house.

'She stepped out under the sky. She ran down the little path to the wicket gate and lifted up her face. "Here I am," she whispered eagerly, and she thought of the infant Samuel. But no God was there, only the bright face of the moon, very near the earth...She kept her eyes on the moon...unconscious of time, surrendering herself to the flood of light. A great peace floated round her and happiness wrapped her... Never would she be lonely. Even when she was quite old, she would have the moon who would go with her' (147-148).

Uttley recalls her 'pagan delight', as she calls it, in the moon's companionship. But the Christian story is just as real and important to her. What emerges so powerfully from this memoir is that in the child's heart and mind there is no conflict between the two, between the 'pagan' and the Christian narratives. Uttley's chapter headed 'Moonlight' is immediately followed by chapters entitled 'December' and 'Christmas Day' which record her joyful engagement in the Christmas story. She is sure that the cattle know it is Christmas and that they kneel on Christmas Eve. 'Down they all went, bowing to the New Saviour *as she bowed to the new moon*' (181) (My italics).

Frank O'Connor's memoir of a deprived Irish childhood *An Only Child* is memorable for its portrait of an indomitable mother, holding her impoverished household together despite the fecklessness of a drunken father. The young O'Connor's circumstances were as appalling as those recalled in Frank McCourt's *Angela's Ashes*, yet there was, he tells us, a spiritual aspect to his dreadfully disadvantaged childhood. But it was far from a 'sunsets and waterfalls' spirituality.

O'Connor discovers his 'spiritual springs'—the term is his—in his reading, especially in boys' magazines, such as *The Gem* and *The Magnet*, and in popular stories of English public school life. The heroes of these tales are the 'invisible presences' who accompany and guide him. (He toyed with 'Invisible Presences' as a title for his memoir). Declan Kibberd comments in his Introduction to the Penguin Classics edition of O'Connor's autobiography.

'"The invisible presences" were those honourable schoolboys who know how to take a punishment without complaint and how they must never betray a friend to the authorities. This code was far removed from the behaviour of boys in the back-streets of Cork. So a split emerged between the child's reading and his world. His fantasies were, however, seldom checked by close involvement with other children and so he was always "half in and half out of the world of reality, like Moses descending the mountain or a dreamer waking"' (Kibberd in O'Connor, 2005).

The boy's paper is 'a sort of promise of better things'. He glances at it under his desk—and here we register the religious image—'as a man in mortal agony will glance at a crucifix' (O'Connor, 2005, 101). O'Connor speaks of this world of the English public schools as his 'spiritual homeland' (110).

Rosemary Sutcliffe and her best friend Jean escape to a world—and find friends there—fashioned, like Frank O'Connor's, from the school stories they read.

'We had only to say, "Let's be Lilian and Diana," and, as though it was a magical formula, step straight into a world that was as real to us as the world of school and parents and cornflakes for breakfast. It was a boarding school world—nothing very unusual or original in that—based heavily on the writings of Angela Brazil and *The Schoolgirls Own*' (Sutcliffe, 1984, 70).

In the East, there is no suggestion—at least, there never used to be— that unseen friends are fanciful. The Indian child, Mulk Raj Anand, had an invisible playmate. His mother catches him in conversation with this unseen companion and, Anand writes,

'with an esoteric belief in the potentialities of the unknown, (she) wondered whether I was only indulging in make-believe or whether I really saw something. For if I really had the power to see something which was invisible to others, I might be a blessed spirit reincarnated through her womb' (Anand 2005, 225).

Noel Sircar's *An Indian Boyhood* requires us to be less dismissive of the reality of a child's 'imaginary' friend. The author, who calls himself Gopal, meets a strange lonely boy in a garden, a boy without friends, who has played no games, and who knows nothing of tops and kites. Our Gopal befriends this mysterious boy and calls him Prince. Prince comes and goes unpredictably and others cannot see him. 'It was not easy,' Sircar recalls in his introduction, 'to distinguish fact from fancy in the bright silence of that garden' (Sircar, 1948).

Norman Goodland's *Sexton's Boy* is an English memoir demanding from us the same 'suspension of disbelief' as our Indian memoirs demand. This marvellous text recalls a childhood in a Hampshire village, where the boy's father is postman, sexton, gravedigger, and clerk. The memoir's gently implied message is that the child—or, at least, this child—inhabits a world requiring a better explanation than most grown-ups provide. 'Why is the wind blowing from that distant hill?' Norman wonders. His father, who knows more than most grown-ups, tells him that it does do because the shepherd has left a gate open. So, sensibly, the child sets off to close it.

Death is familiar to this country child. Nevertheless the spectacle of a funeral sends Norman rigid with fear. He dreads the little house in the churchyard where the bier that bears the coffins is kept. He fears passing the church doors. ('God was inside—listening!') Sometimes the boy plays by himself in the churchyard where his father is working. There one day he meets a boy called Vernon and makes friends with him. The boys play together among the graves. Vernon takes him to his home, a dilapidated cottage where they have fun with an old water-butt. Norman's parents are puzzled by their son's account of this 'Vernon' whom he has befriended. They know everyone in their small community, but they have not heard of a Vernon. Norman describes Vernon to them—and suddenly his parents are afraid.

It is only many years later that Norman learns from his father that indeed there was once a boy in the village named Vernon. His father tells Norman that it was long before he, Norman, was born that Vernon died. His father was himself only a child at the time, but he remembers Vernon, with all his family, perishing in the fire that destroyed their cottage (Goodland, 1967, 7-13).

Few invisible companions of childhood are retained into adulthood, but Richard Church's unseen friend becomes a friend for life. He describes his first encounter with Jesus—none other—and the friendship that followed in *Over the Bridge*. This exceptionally evocative record of the inner life of an unusually sensitive child stands high in our canon of the classical accounts of childhood. *Over the Bridge* is of the first importance to us as a study of the interface of spirituality, religion, and language in childhood. (It is also the testimony of someone who was chronically ill as a child and thus raises the question—which we note but do not pursue in this essay—of the relationship of illness and spirituality in childhood).

Church was born in 1893 and grew up in south London in a close-knit lower middle class family. His father was a postman, a man of eternally sunny disposition but with no artistic or aesthetic interests. Father's one passion was cycling. His elder brother Jack was reserved, inventive, and brilliantly musical. The household resolved around their vivacious ailing mother to whom Richard was intensely devoted.

Richard Church's experience of the unseen companionship of Christ was rooted in his reading of the Bible—which he had begun, aged seven, with the book of Job!—and the Book of Common Prayer (a present from an aunt). Later we shall return to the role of the Bible and liturgy in spiritual nurture. Here we simply note that it was through his reading of these sacred texts—without adult intervention or introduction—that this young child stumbled on Jesus and found in him a friend.

> 'The character, the very physical person, of Jesus began to loom up as a constant acquaintance. He became a companion of my long days at home, and we talked together as freely as though he were a member of the small family' (Church, 1955, 129).

Richard Church's interest in the Bible prompted his family to go to their local Congregational church, but it was not there (under the ministry of a pastor with 'teeth riddled with decay') that he discovered the friendship of Jesus.

Jesus will become still more vividly present to this rare spirit, as Richard Church surely was, when he has to spend time in a sanatorium. There he experiences episodes of intense—even ecstatic—awareness. We shall come to these moments, among other memories of such 'peak experiences' in childhood, in Chapter Six.

Hidden from the wise, revealed to infants

'When I was a child, I spoke like a child, I thought like a child, I reasoned like a child; when I became a man I gave up my childish ways' (1 Corinthians 13.11).

Much must be jettisoned on the path to Christian maturity. But if Jesus is to be believed, not every aspect of childhood is to be abandoned. Paul urges me to grow up, but Jesus tells me to become a child. Treading the tightrope of Christian discipleship means obeying both commands. Paradoxically, the first step towards Christian adulthood is the recovery of childhood. 'You must,' said Jesus to Nicodemus, who was too grown-up for his own good, 'be born again' (John 3.7).

Jesus said that there are things hidden from the wise and intelligent that are revealed to infants (Matthew 11.25). It must be stressed, defying the consensus of critical opinion, that Jesus is here referring to actual children as well as, possibly, to his adult disciples. What is revealed *to* infants—and to young children generally—is then revealed *by* them, at least to those with the humility to notice what these little ones are telling them.

Our memoirs recall a mode of awareness which once was ours. Sadly, a world too much with us has grievously desensitised us to the transcendent. The children who our writers were invite us to open our hearts and minds again to the possibility of worlds beyond the immediately apparent. We dare to recast Paul's words and hear it said to us, 'Let that mind be in you which was also in the child you were'.

Our writers remember ranging across frontiers closed to adults who have left childhood behind. We wholly miss the point if we take these memories as simply delightful examples of the power of a child's imagination. If we hear what Jesus is saying to us, that children perceive things which grown-ups are too clever to notice, then we should find their memories deeply unsettling. Those memories call in question our unexamined assumptions about what is real. They cause a seismic shift in the ground on which we have settled so complacently and for so long. Becoming as a child means recognising that we may have got things badly wrong, that all may not be as it seems.

Does the suggestion that we should seek a child's sense of the transcendent, of worlds beyond this one, mean that we must return to a medieval world-view? If in some respects it does, so be it. Children are no allies of 'the new atheists' and they teach us not be brow-beaten by those who insist that there is nothing beyond the scientifically verifiable.

Recovering childhood means regaining a larger view of the company we keep. 'We are surrounded by a great cloud of witnesses,' says the writer to Hebrews (12.1). Children too are thus surrounded, companioned by those whom others may not see. Sometimes parents apologise for the seriousness with which their children take their invisible friends, as if consorting with the unseen in this fashion were unhealthy. Those taught by Christ that childhood offers a pattern of discipleship will not share this unease. The territory to which children's unseen friends belong, together with the saints and angels, may, alas, be hidden to adults who are too clever by half. But our memoirs tell us that it is a territory frequently visited by children. Adults who have learned from Jesus that they must become as children will seek that country and its company, though the quest will be costly and painful.

We have been struck by the strain of nostalgia suffusing some of our memoirs, notably those of Raine, Reid, and Rowse. To repeat the point, the longing these writers express is not nostalgia *for* childhood. They are not echoing Thomas Gray—'Alas, regardless of their doom the little victims play' (*Ode on a distant prospect of Eton College*). Nor do they come to Thomas Hood's conclusion—'I'm farther off from Heaven than when I was a boy' (*I remember, I remember*). It is not nostalgia *for* childhood but the nostalgia *of* childhood our writers describe. They remember that, even as children, they hankered for 'somewhere else'.

Rabindranath Tagore recalls a cry he heard as a child, a cry coming at dawn from the banks of the river: 'Ferryman, take me across to the other shore!' Already as a child, Tagore sought 'the other shore'. He sought what he called 'the limitless thing called the Outside', the larger reality of which life allows us only occasional and tantalising hints. The yearning, felt as a child, stays with him.

> 'In the bustle of all our work there comes out this cry, "Take me across." "The carter in India sings while driving his cart, "Take me across." The itinerant grocer deals out his goods to his customer and sings, "Take me across."
>
> What is the meaning of this cry? We feel we have not reached our goal; and we know with all our striving and toiling we do not come to the end, we do not attain our goal. Like a child dissatisfied with its dolls, our heart cries, "Not this, not this." But what is that other? Where is the further shore? Is it something else than what we have? Is it somewhere else than where we are? Is it to take rest from all our works, to be relieved from all the responsibilities of life? No, in the very heart of our activities we are seeking for our end. We are crying for "the across", even where we stand' (Tagore, 1913b, 162).

Tagore writes out of the Hindu tradition, but the longing he voices is universal, a craving not solely of the Hindu spirit but of the human spirit. It is a longing, so our memoirs suggest, already felt in childhood. It is also an aspect of the spirit of the child that we have done little to encourage and that has been woefully little explored.

We must wonder what that disposition implies for Christian discipleship. If indeed we are made for more than meets the eye, for God who is our home, then such nostalgia is no longer one of Paul's childish things to be jettisoned when we grow up, but a mark of the mature Christian spirit.

Nurturing the open mind and spirit

Our memoirs provide abundant evidence that William Trevor was right to say that children lead a double life—at least as they emerge from their earliest days when all experience is one. There is the life that conforms, more or less, to the constraints imposed on the child from the outside. Then there is the child's inner life, his or her spiritual life, the life that knows no such constraints and whose richness is evident from our writers' memories. The formal schooling most children receive is almost entirely directed to shaping the former, to moulding young lives so that they conform to society's prevailing assumptions and expectations. The success of such education is assessed by how far the child achieves certain specified quantifiable targets. Such an education may pay lip-service to the notion that there is a spiritual dimension to the child's life, but in practice it is likely to disregard that aspect of who the child is. The consequence is that a child may succeed educationally, according to the only officially recognised criteria of success, but still emerge from his or her schooling spiritually impoverished.

There are immensely important implications for the role of the church in its service to children, to children subjected to educational dogma that conceives of success in narrowly quantitative terms, in the amassment of impressive exam results, for example. The goal of our formation, as Christianity understands it, is the glory of God in a human being made whole. The church affirms as foundational what in the child's formal schooling, apart from token gestures, is wholly disregarded—the spiritual nature of the child. It follows that there must be a fundamental difference between the nurture of the child in the Christian faith, whether at home or at church, and the teaching most children receive at school. The difference lies in that one word—'nurture'. Nurture is the cultivation of what is already there. The church's primary role with children is not to teach them what we know and they don't. As we have seen in this chapter, children— well aware of worlds beyond this one, friends of those whom our eyes are too old and tired to see—are already spiritually attentive to a far higher degree than most adults. Taught by Christ, we recognise that they are our mentors.

CHAPTER 4

The chilo on the cross

s we have seen, for writers such as Raine, Reid, and Rowse, distress
in childhood, at its deepest level, is a kind of homesickness. We are
exiles from Eden, all of us, however that first home is understood.
On this view, the child's inconsolable grief over a lost or broken toy is at root
our primal anguish over our expulsion from paradise. Make what we will
of such a notion, rarely entertained by students of children's spirituality, it
at least offers some explanation for the intensity of the child's despair when
what is loved is lost. The present writer feels to this day how devastated he
was when, as a seven-year-old, he saw his leather football—a rare wartime
gift—roll under the front wheel of a bus. James Kirkup remembers his
desolation one Christmas when an older child ripped in half a paper chain
he had made. 'I was in despair. It was dreadful to think that the most
beautiful thing I had ever made was broken, and could not be mended'
(Kirkup, 1957, 131). Such despair is not disproportionate if it is born of the
deep knowledge that there is no going back to where we belong.

Many of our writers recall times of deep distress in childhood, but
not all of them have the courage to revisit those early afflictions. Eileen
Elias is brave enough to do so. Her memoir *On Sundays we wore white* is
a record of a superficially happy childhood but it includes an extended
and unflinching account of an inner world of terror of which most adults
would choose to forget. She writes,

'I wonder how any grown-ups understand the enormous cloud of
fear which can at any moment loom up to darken a small child's
sunniest day? Children are happy enough on the surface; but they
have unplumbed depths of dread and anxiety that nobody knows
about except themselves'.

Now that she comes to speak of these terrors—the spiders 'that were sin itself crawling across the floor'—words do not fail her, but it was otherwise when she felt herself buried alive beneath them. She screamed and screamed until someone came but, she tells us, 'I was totally unable to communicate to them the terror that had filled my dream' (Elias, 1978, 91-103).

Leonard Woolf who, as husband of Virginia, was witness of another's deep affliction, is one of the few of our writers to join with Elias in asking why little children too should be prone to such distress. 'I have pointed out,' he writes, 'that the apparently innate and profound unhappiness of the human infant, who will go into loud paroxysms of misery without provocation, is unknown in the young of other animals'. Woolf would have dismissed the notion—axiomatic to Raine, Reid, and Rowse—that the child is crying for some irrecoverable paradise. But he has no alternative explanation. He can only speak of 'this primeval pessimism of man' (Leonard Woolf 1962, 26).

In Chapter Six we shall look back with our writers on the experiences of intense joy, momentary but overwhelming, that they recall from their childhood. At such exultant times they were touched by the transcendent. We shall dwell on such ecstatic memories and, with our writers, we shall wonder what they mean. But we must not forget that such experiences had their dreadful obverse.

Leonard Woolf—to stay with him—describes how in his fifth year he first experienced 'a wave of that profound, cosmic melancholia which is hidden in every human heart and can be heard at its best—or should one say worst?—in the infant crying in the night and with no language but a cry'. He tells how, on his return with his family one year from their annual summer holiday, he rushes out into their back garden. He notices that the ivy, which covered the garden walls, was now draped in spider-webs, each with a motionless spider, large or small, squatting at its centre. For the rest of his life Woolf will remember the effect on him of what he saw.

'Suddenly my whole mind and body seemed to be overwhelmed in melancholy. I did not cry, though there were, I think, tears in my eyes; I had experienced for the first time, without understanding it, that sense of cosmic unhappiness which comes upon us when those that look out of the windows are darkened, when the daughters of music are laid low, the doors are shut in the street, the sound of the grinding is low, the grasshopper is a burden and desire fails.' (Leonard Woolf, 1962, 27-28)

This will not be the last time that, while still a child, Leonard Woolf feels 'the burden of a hostile universe weigh down on (his) spirit'. He cites Thomas Traherne, another who had known deep dread in early years.

'Another time in a lowering and sad evening, being alone in the field, when all things were dead and quiet, a certain want and horror fell upon me, beyond imagination. The unprofitableness and silence of the place dissatisfied me; its wideness terrified me: from the utmost ends of the earth fears surrounded me' (Traherne, cited in Woolf, 1962, 29).

We must return to these dark places before this chapter is done.

Survivors' testimonies

Children suffer spiritually. But, of course, not only spiritually. The memories of 'slum childhoods' we have cited are of material hardship. Such hardship is not wholly a thing of the past. In the twenty-first century, in the so-called developed world, there are plenty of impoverished urban neighbourhoods where households with many children have to make do on very little. As for the less developed world, harrowing images of hungry children bring home to us—or at least bring to our homes—what are the child's primary needs. So too do the pictures, though many are too graphic to be screened, of the child victims of today's wars. *Save the Children* reports that one in four of the world's children is physically stunted and that in developing countries this figure is as high as one in three. These are children, we are told, 'whose bodies and brains have failed to develop properly because of malnutrition' (Save the Children Annual Report, 2012).

Such children do not go on to write memoirs of their childhood. Nor do terminally ill children. We have no autobiographies from adults recalling what it was to be a child who knew that he or she would die very soon, though some of those children themselves have spoken from the heart. (Many such moving testimonies are included Fred Epstein's *If I get to five* (Epstein, 2003)). The life-stories which are the present book's database were written by survivors, by men and women who made it through.

Among the survivors are Jews who lived to tell the tale of their suffering under the Nazis. (Though of course the most famous account of childhood under the Nazis comes to us not from a survivor but from a victim (*The Diary of a Young Girl*, Anne Frank, 1952)). I mention just one such memoir. Charles Hannam's *Boy in your Situation* is a closely observed account of growing up as a Jewish boy in Essen in the 1930s. Hannam was a pampered child of a wealthy banking family. He is remarkably frank about his lying, his regular stealing from his parents, and his taste for the scatological. But his memoir is also chilling documentation of his experience of growing anti-Semitism at school and of how what at first is merely irritating becomes a source of spiritual distress. Before long it all becomes much worse, until he escapes just in time on a *Kindertransport* (Hannam, 1977). *Boy in your Situation* is a sombre account of mounting darkness, the darkness gathering in a child's world and a child's spirit.

Charles Hannam survives, but untold numbers of children—whether victims of a vicious dictatorship, or of hunger, or of war, or of preventable disease, or of an aggressive illness—do not survive. In discussing the spiritual distress of childhood, we must never overlook the fact that it is physical distress and material deprivation that blights and curtails so many young lives. We may well wonder whether we may even dare speak of the 'spiritual development' of the hungry child. We have learned from our memoirs that there is no separating the spiritual from the sensory in childhood. Chronic hunger and spiritual distress are a single affliction for innumerable children world-wide. The best we can do spiritually for a hungry child is to obey the Lord's command, 'Give her something to eat' (Mark 5.43).

Our memoirs, we say, are *survivors'* testimonies. But some of those survivors write of wounds that, long into adult life, are still unhealed. We are bound to mention those who suffered sexual abuse as children, abuse sometimes perpetuated over many years. Michael Clemenger's *Everybody Knew* (Clemenger, 2012) may stand as one title—alas, among numerous others—recalling such affliction.

Spiritual distress

Even when their material needs are amply met, children suffer inwardly, their suffering compounded by their incapacity to express it. That is why it is important that we listen to adults who at last are able to utter the anguish for which as children they had 'no language but a cry'. Many of their recollections will resonate with those of their adult readers. We have been there too. But, unlike most of us, they find words to speak of their affliction. Those words are often painful to read. The witness of our memoirs to the spiritual distress of children corrects any inclination we might have to imagine the days of childhood to have been passed in unbroken sunshine.

The term 'spiritual distress' comes from the nursing world. It is an approved nursing diagnosis and has been defined by the North American Nursing Diagnosis Association (NADA) as 'a disruption in the life principle that pervades a person's entire being and that integrates and transcends one's biological and psychological nature'. But clearly spiritual distress, so defined, is not only experienced by those needing to be nursed. Children do not have to be hospitalised to be distressed in spirit. The key word in the NADA definition is 'pervades'. We shall see how the spiritual distress that children suffer takes over their whole being. The gift of detachment, the capacity to stand apart from what they are going through, is not yet available to them.

Fear of the dark

The primal affliction of childhood is fear. Geoffrey Dennis's childhood world teems with the terrifying. The catalogue of 'fears' begins, understandably enough, with 'Cane', an instrument his sadistic father loved to use But as it unfolds, the list becomes stranger. Dogs frighten him, but so too do the logs of felled trees in the park. So also do dolls' eyes, with which the little girls chased him. There is so much to be frightened of—a hunchback sitting on a park seat near him, a picture of an octopus, the vague threat of the bogey man, among many other horrors (Dennis, 1957, 87-93).

Reading such a memoir reminds us how irrational some of our childhood fears were. (I recall my own infant terror of vehicles with three wheels.) Roads glinting and sparkling in the sun after rain stir in the young Richard Wollheim 'the deepest, darkest melancholy'. Their effect is on him is to convince him, 'beyond anything that hope could counter, that life would never again have anything to offer' (Wollheim, 2004, 45).

The worst fears of childhood, however, are not of the specific and identifiable, but of the unknown. Geoffrey Dennis, to return to this writer of strange prose, is in dread:

'of a blank, a void, no name or shape to it, the deep-down Nothing. Of the Universe... of its space and time everlastingness. Already grooming itself as my private shape of the Terror unescapable ultimate: ETERNITY' (Dennis, 1957, 87-93).

The most frequently attested form of spiritual distress recalled from childhood and the most debilitating is fear of the dark—and fear of what darkness brings, not least the nightmares that mercifully most of us in adult years are spared.

'In childhood there was this dream,
Recurrent and unyielding
I was in a dark mill, or I was the mill,
The grindstones were grinding, with nothing
    At all to grind, they groaned and groaned
    And when I woke, the dull heavy sound
    Went on. I would wait for it to stop.
    But in the end I had to call my mother'
Night-light (Enright, 1973).

Christopher Fitz-Simon was born into an extraordinary Irish family, with Daniel O'Connell, campaigner for Catholic emancipation on one side, and Ulster Protestants on the other. His childhood coincided with the Second World War. *Eleven Houses* is a memoir of his family's progress through the succession of houses that, each in turn, became his childhood home. The boy accompanies his father on a shooting expedition. A snipe is brought down but not killed until his father thrusts a long pin through its head. At night the bird returns to haunt him.

'It became alive again in my hands and fluttered and fluttered till its wings were beating my face, beating and beating, and I couldn't speak or cry because the words got trapped in my throat and all that came out was a hiss, just like the snipe's last breath and I was shaking and shaking' (Fitz-Simon, 2007, 34).

Eileen Elias recalls the terror of soul she suffered when she was made to climb the stairs after dark to fetch her Aunt Jane's spectacles. 'Fear of the dark,' she writes, 'must surely be one of the primeval fears of our race; no child I have ever known has been without it' (Elias, 1978, 100-101). Most of us experienced such fear when we were small, but not all of us have the courage to relive it as our writers do. Here I cite some few further recollections from many such memories that could be quoted.

Elisaveta Fen lived in terror of the dark corner of her bedroom 'where unnameable things might be hiding'.

'In the daylight it was occupied by an ordinary low cupboard filled with a chaotic assortment of picture books and toys, but at night it became the lair of some formless supernatural creature, neither human nor animal, hideously furtive and black as darkness itself. It was best not to look at it for, if you did, it began to stir, as if about to crawl out. Yet it was difficult not to look: it exercised a magnetic attraction' (Fen, 1961, 50).

Alone in bed for his first night in Larling's Old Rectory, their new home, five year old 'Col' Middleton Murry sees the curtains of his room 'tremble as though they were alive'. Clearly there is something about to pounce on him. His sister hears his terrified cries and comes to his room. She seizes the fire tongs and attacks the quivering curtains. Then she tucks her little brother into bed and kisses him good night. She is all of six years old (Murry, 1975, 40).

Jeanne Ivaldi's family came from Russia but she grew up in America. She tells us her recurrent dream: 'At night I dream I am being chased. I run as far as I can but I am falling behind the others who are far ahead of me. Each time I look over my shoulder, the pursuer looms larger. It's a man! It's Frankenstein!' (Ivaldi, 2001, 24).

Dorothea Rutherford grew up in Reval (now Talinn), the capital of Estonia, at the turn of the twentieth century. Her story of her childhood, in which she is the little girl Liesbeth, deserves to be better known. Like most children, Liesbeth is prey to night-time terrors.

'The worst is when (Liesbeth) happens to wake up in the middle of the night. It is so strange and silent, as though everybody had died... An indescribable sadness overcomes her and she has to cry. She lies in the dark, listens to her own sobbing and feels very sorry for herself. She is alone...nobody can help her...She is alone abandoned in a dark wilderness, and who knows what is lying in wait for her? It may be the Angel of Death, the big dark one in a floating robe with a long palm whom she saw in a book. She had told God that she wanted to come to Him in heaven and now he is taking her at her word' (Rutherford, 1955, 10-11).

For many of the world's children, night is terrifying because it is the time when evil spirits and ghosts are abroad. Taha Hussein, born in 1889, writing of his Egyptian childhood, describes the fears faced by the boy he was.

'He knew full well if he uncovered his face in the course of the night or exposed any of the extremities of his body, they would be at the mercy of one of the numerous evil sprites which inhabited every part of the house, filling every nook and cranny...But his greatest terror of all was of persons who, in his imagination, stood in the doorway of the room and blocked it and began to make various noises...He firmly believed he had no protection from all these terrifying apparitions and horrible noises unless he wrapped himself up inside the coverlet from head to toe' (Hussein, 1932, 3).

Fear of the dark can be a daytime experience. Alison Uttley—the 'Susan' of *A Country Child*—had to walk four miles to school each day. Her journey took her through 'the dark wood' which terrified her. 'No one ever knew Susan's fears, she never even formulated them to herself, except as "things"... Something was behind the oak tree, hidden, lurking, and all the leaves watched her approach' (Uttley, 1936, 3).

For some of our children, their dread of the dark is only made worse by what they were taught about religion.

Helen Thomas Flexner, the youngest daughter of a highly intelligent American Quaker family, was born in 1871. In her early years she grew up in terror of Satan. This constant fear was the fault of her devout mother who, with the best intentions, had told her little girl to repeat the prayer 'Get thee behind me, Satan' as a means of controlling her temper.

'Alas! Satan thus frequently addressed was as real to me as any other. Even in the sunny, well-inhabited nursery where he was invisible, his presence behind my back made being virtuous far from a comfortable state...At night-time Satan grew very bold. The whole house was haunted by his presence'. (Flexner, 1940, 2-3)

When she is very small Eleanor Acland's horror of the dark is both of 'the nothingness which provides no defence against the clutch of fear' and of 'the enormous almost shapeless slugs which plastered themselves along the floor and heave themselves up the side of her cot'. When she is older other night-time fears supersede these, above all the fear—now that she has a bedroom of her own—that she has been banished to this lonely room because of her naughtiness. Her fears are intensified by 'beliefs implanted in her in the name of religion', by what she has been taught of 'the all-seeing, all-judging Eye, the fire of hell that he could not or would not quench, and the washing in blood' (Acland, 1935, 75-84).

More must be said, unfortunately, about the malign influence of 'bad religion' on the child's spirit. This is the melancholy theme I take up in Chapter Seven.

Haunted childhoods

As we have seen, for many children the boundary between the seen and the unseen is blurred. Such children are sometimes troubled by fearful presences haunting the borderlands of their awareness. James Kirkup is terrified when he is 'bunked up' on to the churchyard wall and told ghost stories. These terrors return to torment him at night.

'Before I learned to recognise the sound of my own heart beating, I would lie awake in the darkness listening to the pulse of blood in my head, and think it was the tramp of ghostly feet' (Kirkup, 1957, 28-29).

To suggest that such children 'imagine things' trivialises their experience. Their fear is all too real, whether what arouses it is wholly a product of their imagination or, say, a sheet flapping on a clothes-line. John Raynor, son of a housemaster at Westminster school, grew up in an old house close to the Abbey. In his *A Westminster Childhood*, one of the richest of our memoirs, he writes of his 'profound psychic receptivity' as a child (Raynor, 1973, 16). He is fearful of the ghosts that possess his 'tormented old house' (49) and is moved to horror by an unearthly sound that regularly haunts his sleepless nights (19-21).

Laurie Lee's classic account of his Cotswold childhood powerfully evokes childhood terrors.

'The yard and the village manifested themselves at first through magic and fear. Projections of their spirits and of my hallucinations sketched in the first blanks with demons. The thumping of heart-beats which I heard in my head was no longer the unique ticking of a private clock but the marching of monsters coming in from outside.'

Perhaps the most terrifying of the monstrous beings haunting little Laurie's childhood were 'the Old Men' who 'lived in the walls in floors, and down the lavatory; who watched and judged us and were obviously gods gone mouldy' (Lee, 1962, 28).

The playwright and biographer Brian Thompson remembers a disastrous family holiday in Hastings. His father takes him to a small aquarium exhibiting hideous 'denizens of the deep'.

'Nothing dredged from the deep can be so terrible as to frighten someone in balance with the world but I felt a deep shuddering revulsion in that sweaty cabin, the memory of which has never left me. All that was bad about us was metaphorised by those gaping mouths and bulging empty eyes: I felt myself go hot and cold and clung to the trestles on which the show was laid out. A huge meaty hand landed on my shoulder and a fisherman caught me before I fell' (Thompson, 2006, 146-147).

Here a child meets by day monsters whose proper realm is night. The fear of the dark and of the malignities that that emerge from it, whether after dark or after daybreak, is a distress of spirit surely as acute as any suffered by the saints during their souls' dark nights.

Every reason to be fearful

Of course children experience spiritual distress for more understandable reasons.

There is the distress of being teased. Little Serghei Aksakoff is teased by his uncles. They tell him that an imperial edict requires him to serve in the army and that their friend Volkoff proposes to marry Serghei's beloved sister and to carry her off to war. The adult Aksakoff comments, 'Here lay the trouble, that a child cannot clearly distinguish the boundary between jest and earnest' (Aksakoff, 1923, 105).

Some of our memoirs recall the misery of the child of the unhappy marriage. Emma Smith and her twin siblings live in fear of the rage of their embittered unsmiling father, who, they sense, blames them for the disappointment of his life. Once he was a war hero. Once he might have become an artist. Now he is imprisoned in a bank (Emma Smith, 2008, 132). Emma's distress is compounded by her inability to tell her mother, who suffers equally from this unhappy man, how much she loves her (144-145).

Brian Thompson, who was so terrified by the unspeakable creatures he met in a Hastings aquarium, has worse to contend with at home. His *Keeping Mum* is the record of a child's best efforts to cope with an appallingly dysfunctional mother. 'Don't ever ask me for nothing, Brian,' she says, 'because I haven't got it to give' (Brian Thompson, 2006, 143).

Several writers have terrible memories of their early schooldays. To be sure, some of these memories, such as the recollections of Serghei Aksakoff and Juliette Adam, are of conditions from which we like to think we have moved on.

On his first day at school, little Serghei is appalled by the appearance in his classroom of 'the school-keepers', summoned to thrash a delinquent.

'Three of them came in, armed with bundles of birch rods, and set to work to flog the boys who were kneeling down. To me this scene was terrible and disgusting: as soon as it began, I shut my eyes and stuffed my fingers into my ears. My first instinct was to run away, but I was shaking all over and dared not move' (Aksakoff, 1923, 118).

The French writer Juliette Adam, born in 1836, was known also by her maiden name Juliette Lamber. As a child she was torn between her parents—who were themselves at war with each other—and her grandparents. Her father was a revolutionary and an atheist; her grandmother, who brought her up, was a royalist and a devout catholic.

On arriving with her grandmother at school she is greeted by Madame Dufey, the schoolmistress. ('She had mustaches, I thought her ugly and she terrified me'). Madame Dufey carries Juliette off in her arms and her grandmother leaves her. 'Nothing,' she will recall, 'had ever seemed to me so frightful as this abandonment'. She hits out at 'an under-mistress' who has shaken her because she has refused to stop crying. As a punishment she is locked in an attic (Adam, 1903, 68-80).

In many other memoirs of childhood, the first day at school is as unhappy a memory as it was for Serghei Aksakoff and Juliette Adam. Much in these memories would lend support to all that John Bowlby has taught us about the damage done to a child by abrupt separation from the familiar caregiver (Bowlby 1969, 1973, 1980).

Emanuel Litvinoff grew in the 1930s in a crowded ghetto in Bethnal Green in London's East End, a community of Jews who had fled from persecution in the Russian empire. His memoir is one of the numerous autobiographies of life in a Jewish family in London's East end. When Emanuel was four, his mother took him to school—and left him there.

'When I looked round my mother had gone, disappeared... Incoherent with shock, I spent the entire day swollen-faced and blubbering, kicking out like a caged animal at anyone unwise enough to try to pacify me' (Litvinoff, 1993, 31).

Ted Walker, who grew up in rural Sussex, has similar memories of being abandoned by his mother—for so it felt to him—on being taken to school for the first time.

'When I looked around, my mother was gone. I did not cry; but the fast-inflating bladder of a sob made such a painful obstruction in my chest that I was not able to murmur, or to breathe deep, or even ponder my misery...I turned my head and looked across the yard to the black railings where I thought my mother might be. She was not there. Every desertion and betrayal I have suffered in my life since has been measured in terms of that moment's despair' (Walker 1982, 31).

Bryan Magee writes of the primal grief that overtakes the classroom of children, of whom he is one, when they are discarded by their mothers on the first day of school.

'There we were, thirty-five of us, sitting in rows at our tiny desks, crying our eyes out, the tears streaming down our faces, sobbing and yelling at the tops of our voices. It was the first consciously traumatic experience I ever had, but it was a powerful group experience too, and it has remained with me as one of the most vivid memories from any period of my life' (Magee, 2003, 41).

For some children, the distress of their schooldays does not end with the first day of their first term. The unathletic Edward Blishen, one day to become an acclaimed novelist, remembers being required to join in a relay-race in his district school sports. 'I was overwhelmed by the sheer horror of it. Terror rose, a great chain reaction of gulping and gaspings, in my throat' (Blishen, 1978, 72).

Worst of all for Blishen—as, alas, for so many children—is the experience of being bullied. Edward Blishen writes of 'the trivial, eternal cruelty of schoolboys', of 'the plain barbarism' of life at school, of the dark cellars beneath the school building where big boys removed little boys' trousers. He remembers, amongst the other afflictions, 'the agony in that blackness, of crouching in your underpants, wondering if you would have time, before the next lesson began, to collect your trousers from the dusty tangle at the entrance' (90-91).

Colin Middleton Murry was known as 'Midge' by the boarders at Thretford Grammar School where he was mercilessly bullied by the bigger boy Reggie and his gang. To 'get Midge' was one of Reggie's favourite pastimes. The physical suffering 'Col' experienced was nothing short of torture, but he sees what was subsequently inflicted on him was as still worse.

> 'Sometimes Reggie would go to work on me with a pin, sometimes with a piece of string, sometimes with his bare hands. He had a genuine talent for devising tortures and one of my fingernails is still mis-shapen from a pin wound which went septic. But I could stand almost any amount of physical pain, and Reggie, realizing this, soon changed his tactics. I was sent to Coventry... I became a pariah, an untouchable, and I began to believe that the endless night was truly closing in upon me' (Murry, 1975, 95-96).

As we read these memories of the spiritual distress of the bullied, we may well reflect on the spiritual plight of the bully. Elisaveta Fen cannot understand why God allows animals to suffer so much, yet she admits to joining with other children in teasing Vitya, a boy who stammers (Fen, 1961, 165-166). Bullying, the infliction of pain with the purpose of gaining pleasure, clearly poses problems for our understanding of children's spirituality.

In *Sun before Seven*, Charles Higgins (writing under the pseudonym of Ian Dall) describes growing up in the 1890s in Belgrano, then a few miles from Buenos Aires, now a suburb of the city. His happy childhood ends when, not yet seven, he is sent away to boarding-school. Ian Dall revisits the dark places of the spirit to which he was brought during his time at this school. His unflinching description of the afflictions visited on the child he was and the inner anguish that this sensitive little boy experienced make for heart-breaking reading. It is also essential reading, for Dall has the courage to recall, as only few of our writers do (Eileen Elias among them), just how extreme is the spiritual torment a child can suffer. His account of what he went through closes as he climbs into a 'fiddle–case' in a cupboard in the school's music-room. We wonder whether, driven almost out of his mind by all he has suffered, he is hallucinating. 'The lid shut down on life,' he tells us, 'and I was dead' (Dall, 1936, 201-217).

One thing at least young bullies do for us. They deliver us from any idealisation of childhood. (Some of today's children will one day write their memoirs. It is distressing to reflect that among them will be those who recall a peculiarly vicious form of the cruelty children can inflict on one another, that of 'cyber-bullying'.)

In our memoirs we meet children who take pleasure in hurting others. But at the same time those memoirs forbid any notion of childhood as innately sinful. Hal Porter is well aware of the equivocal moral condition of the child.—'I am born a good boy,' he writes, 'good but not innocent, this two-sided endowment laying me wide open to assaults of evil not only from without but also from within' (Porter, 1963, 9). The children of our texts are children inescapably bound up in a web of life shot through with sin and tragedy. The bully and the bullied are both victims.

The valley of the shadow of death

A large subject meriting a study of its own is children's early experience of death. A number of our writers describe what it meant to them as children when someone close to them died. Most children's first and continuing response is bewilderment.

Leo Tolstoy's account of the death of his mother must be among the most remarkable of such recollections. Tolstoy was only two when his mother died and, like much in his *Childhood, Boyhood, and Youth*, his account must be read as largely fictional. Yet it is not to be dismissed as untruthful. Tolstoy recognises the complexity and the confusion of a child's reaction to death. As always in Tolstoy—and as in few other writers— acute subjective awareness and exact observation go together. Tolstoy's description, too long to quote, is of a child not so overwhelmed by grief that he is unaware that he must be seen to be grieving. He notes the child's perplexity as he attempts to relate the lifeless body to the living mother he remembers. He recalls how the child is distracted by curiosity about others crowding round the open coffin and what they are wearing. At the service held in the home before the subsequent funeral in church, he is anxious about how to keep his trousers clean when he is obliged to kneel.

Significantly, it was the *smell* of death—'what the strong oppressive smell was that, mingling with the incense, filled the whole room'—that brought home to him 'the bitter truth' of what had happened. It was that, he tells us, which finally 'filled my soul with despair' (Tolstoy, 1930 107-115).

Mikey Cuddihy's remarkable *A Conversation about Happiness* is a more recent memoir to explore what it does to a child when his or her mother dies. Mikey grew up in New York 'in a glamorous world of parties, perfume and booze-filled affection'. At the age of ten Mikey's mother was killed in a car crash and Mikey was brought to London. She is sent to board at A. S. Neill's anarchic Summerhill where she 'aches for her mother ceaselessly'. Mother had been 'erratic, drunk, disorderly, but adored.' 'She's my mother,' says Cuhiddy, 'and I miss her.' This memoir is exceptional, not so much as a record of the immediate experience of bereavement but as a study of a continuing sense of loss, of the pain that goes on. The forlorn child sits on the wall of Summerhill, but 'no one who cares ever shows up and the one person she craves is long gone.' 'She will never come,' are the book's final words (Cudidihy, 2014, 262).

The death of Mikey's mother, child of an affluent family, was sudden and shocking. Death was a more familiar event in poor families—as, of course, in the poor places of the world, it still is. William Woodruff was the child of a Lancashire weaving community. He grew up in the early 1920s in a family that was always poor but which, with the closure of the mills, descended into utter destitution. A still-born baby brother is born. For William, the baby is a white doll with blood on it. No one tells him what had happened to his brother 'except that he'd died', a response that means nothing to him. When the tiny coffin is taken out of the house, the boy asks where his baby brother is going. To be told that he is going 'straight to heaven' only deepens his bewilderment. The baby's death, Woodruff tells us, leaves him afraid (Woodruff, 1993, 58-60).

But death does not always make a deep impact when a child is very small. It is sometimes recalled as something that disturbs the adult's world more than the child's. After Ted Walker's baby sister Ruth died—she was only three weeks old—his mother would regularly take him in his push-chair to the cemetery in North Lancing. There she would tend the little grave.

'As she knelt with her trowel, sometimes she would be in floods of tears; and then, abruptly, I would be clasped tight to the black, shiny curls of her Astrakhan collar. I was blithe, with no sense then of the little girl whose death (whatever *death* was) caused my mother so much anguish. All I felt, when she released me and wiped her tears from her cheek and mine...was the first, vague glimmering that tears were not only associated with falling over and grazing your knees. Something there certainly was that seemed to menace the grown-up world; it occasioned choked mutterings, the hiding of faces, sudden withdrawals from my presence, surprising and painful bear-hug embraces I had not solicited' (Walker, 1992, 6).

Death touches older children more closely. Mulk Raj Anand remembers his bewilderment and fear when his little brother Prithvi dies.

'There descended one day the shadow of an invisible, frightening thing called "Death"...as I realised that he often used to be lying there where I lay in my mother's lap, but was not there now, I felt my mother was not my own and I was terribly frightened. I closed my eyes against Prithvi's face that seemed to becoming towards me from a far land where he had gone, nearer and nearer, for I was sure that he would return' (Anand, 2005, 18-20).

We notice that for this child death is experienced as the loss of his mother as much as the loss of his brother.

For children older still the impact of a death can be much more devastating. Kathleen Raine tells us that the sudden death from meningitis on Easter Day of her eleven-year old cousin—she herself was a year older—'put an end to his childhood, and, as it seems, to my own'.

> 'The horror that took possession of me was, literally, a darkening of the light. The light was filled with blackness, the light itself was emptied of light...For me the bright Easter sun was dark, shedding blackness.'

Raine probes this experience unflinchingly, asking whether she herself had been possessed by her cousin's banished spirit.

> 'It was as if I as well as he had died from the living world and that bright Easter sunlight' (Raine, 1973, 61).

Leo Tregenza recalls growing up in Cornwall, in Mousehole and then in Paul, in the early twentieth century. His *Harbour Village* is a compelling, affectionate account of village life, no less fascinating that so much in such communities has changed. The fishermen, the moods and perils of the sea, the Wesleyan chapel and its occasional comedies—all are lovingly recalled. The foreground is the vivid detail of the immediacies of daily life, the background—understated but deeply felt—is a larger reality, affirmed but not explained.

Leo was just a little older than his sister Mary when, soon after her eighth birthday, she died. Leo's relationship to Mary, the youngest of the family, was close and protective and he finds it hard to accept the fact of her death. The cemetery where she is buried is very near to the school playground and in the weeks and months after her death he frequently visits her grave, reading and rereading the inscription on the cross above it. As his visits become rarer he feels that he is deserting her.

'With the exercise of what power of thought I had I would try once more to annul her death, appealing even to the magic of the wide day to restore the past and let us start again from the happy, blessed state of yesterday'

Shortly after his sister's death, young Leo has a dream in which she appears to him. 'Are you in heaven?' he asks. 'Yes,' she replies—and that is all (Tregenza, 1977, 109-112).

Bryan Magee learns that he will have to die one day when his mother explains lines from the poem with which *Alice through the Looking Glass* begins.

> 'We are but older children, dear,
> Who fret to find our bedtime near.'

Young Bryan resists the bitter truth of the poem.

'I didn't want to die. But the more I reflected on it, the more I realised that I was going to whether I wanted to or not. And then I started to feel sorry for myself. I was swept by a sense of unutterable sadness, real grief, true mourning for myself. I was confronting the loss of everything. And there was nothing I could do about it. Tears came into my eyes every time I thought about it' (Magee, 2003, 133-134).

Perhaps it was to be expected of one who will become a distinguished philosopher, that his first questions about what it means to die are prompted, not by the shock of a death in his own circle, but by reflection on a literary text.

The dark night of the child's soul.

The sickly child Richard Church has been put on a train in London in the custody of an unfeeling nurse. They are destined for a sanatorium in Kent.

'My despair was too great for me to try to explain...So I said nothing and subsided into my inner darkness, that night of the soul which during childhood can be as absolute as it is short-lived' (Church, 1955, 154).

'I subsided into... the night of the soul.' There is a darkness, that some of our authors entered, deeper even than the darkness at the head of the stairs or of the unlit room. These writers remember how as children they sensed—long before they had the concepts or language to speak of it—that our human condition is fundamentally tragic.

Ralph Glasser, Gorbals child, is devastated when his close friend Charlie leaves with his family for Russia. This is in the 1930s when many supposed that the Soviet Union was the Promised Land. Ralph recalls his friend's sweetness of nature. When a gang try to pick a fight with him, Charlie's 'stillness of spirit, his solid innocence, left them nothing to oppose' (Glasser, 1986, 3). When his friend leaves—and he will never see him again— Ralph is overwhelmed by a the sense of 'a capricious, implacably evil force, always lying in wait, of a world deaf to the pleadings of simple humanity, as a child always sees its logic to be' (16).

Bertram Smith describes how his generally happy childhood was sometimes plunged into deep darkness.

'No ultimate expression of distress—"plunged in despair", "lost to all hope" could be too strong for those dark moments when they came...It might be caused by disappointment or injustice; by a sense of not being wanted, an outcast; or, again, by a tragedy and a queer, overwhelming sympathy and tenderness—a most uncomfortable, a haunting thing, not at all compatible with one's usual manly disregard of other people's feelings, which worked the more inward havoc because it had to be suppressed' (Bertram Smith, 1920, 105-106).

The philosopher Bryan Magee describes 'the most disturbing' of the nightmares he regularly suffered.

'Although I was asleep, my whole being would be taken over by a supercharged sense of loss, limitless loss, as if all the sorrow of the world were mine and irreparable, a cosmic bereavement that was forever impossible to rectify. I would lie in bed convulsed with sobbing, moaning, groaning, gulping, crying my eyes out, and yet all the time I was asleep' (Magee, 2003, 129).

Spiritual directors teach their clients that 'the dark night of the soul', such as St John of the Cross entered, comes far down the road on our long journey to God. Those just starting on the spiritual path are unlikely to encounter it. They may well experience 'darkness' of different kinds and of various degrees, but such darkness is most unlikely to be that which the saints experience shortly before being blessed by the vision of God. The dark night of the soul is certainly not for children.

Is it not? We must again ponder the implications of Jesus's teaching about children, that those who receive a child receive him, and that those who receive him receive the one who sent him. We brood once more on Christ's enigmatic word that what is hidden from us, as we make our painful way back to God, is revealed to children (Matthew 11.25-26).

In the light of such teaching we begin to sense a profound correspondence between the passion of Jesus and the distress of the child. It is an equivalence rarely recognised and little explored. The child fearful of the dark and the Christ of God dreading Calvary are very close. We interpret the experience of the child, who senses that 'all the sorrow of the world' is his, in the light—in the 'dark light'—of the Servant who bears our infirmities and carries our diseases. The more we ponder the two images—the suffering child and the crucified Christ—the closer they come to each other until finally they merge. The child in terror of what waits for him at the head of the stairs is Christ in Gethsemane. Christ crying from Calvary 'Why have you forsaken me?' is the child calling for the mother who has deserted him on the first day of school. It is the child who is on the cross. It is Jesus who is left alone in the nursery, in 'anguish without answer'.

Because Jesus identified himself with children, I have dared to suggest that memories of childhood disclose truth about Jesus. If they do, then the recollections of spiritual distress in our memoirs, give us an inkling, if no more, of the affliction Jesus embraced in accepting our condition.

Darkness, discipleship, and nurture

Jesus tells me that I must become a child if I am to enter his kingdom. Does this mean that I must re-enter the darkness which a child suffers? If I listen to the saints who speak from their dark night, the unwelcome answer is that, unless I am spared, I must. The child I must become is the child on the cross. The memories we have shared in this chapter should finally deliver us from the fantasy that becoming a child means no more than the cultivation of what we see as the endearing and attractive qualities of childhood. That notion is an absurd misconception. Indeed it is a plain impossibility. The child I must become is the afflicted child, who may or may not display the attributes of childhood that adults find appealing.

The pastoral implications of our harrowing recollections of spiritual distress are far-reaching. Those who work with children's are rightly encouraged to make sure that children's activities are enjoyable. But it was not for our entertainment that the Word was made flesh and something more than a sense of fun is needed to engage with the darker realities of what it is to be a child.

We hear the words of Jesus, 'Whoever receives one such child in my name receives me' (Mark 9.37). Those words might well be written across the story of each of the suffering children we have met in this chapter. 'Receive' in the New Testament is a rich word. It means bearing the burdens of the one who is welcomed. To take up Christ's cross is to take up the child's cross—the cross carried by the children our writers once were—and to stay with them in their darkness, however long the night.

More is required of us than giving up After-Eights for Lent.

CHAPTER 5

'I AM THE WIND'—NATURE AND SPIRIT

Our spirituality, our 'awareness of the other and the beyond', is inborn. That is how we are. But like any other human capacity our spirituality needs to be nourished if it is to thrive. Just as some environments are healthier than others for our physical growth, so too some are more conducive to our spiritual well-being. Many of our memoirs suggest that the spirit of the child flourishes when the child lives close to nature. In this chapter we shall share the memories of writers for whom, as children, the natural world was a daily delight.

We are spiritually enriched as children by contact with nature. The supreme statement of this principle is found in the first two books of William Wordsworth's *The Prelude*. It could be said that subsequent autobiographical studies of childhoods shaped by nature are, at best, no more than postscripts to this great work. We need to return to *The Prelude* repeatedly to rid our minds of over-simplified accounts of a 'Wordsworthian' view of the child and nature. We have been far too long distracted by those daffodils, charming as they are. We reread those opening books of *The Prelude* to taste again the thrill of great poetry but we need to do so too to *understand* what we are reading. *The Prelude* is an electrifying work but it is also a demanding and, in some passages, a dense work, a product of profound philosophical reflection as well as of extraordinary poetic power.

A discussion of *The Prelude* would be far too ambitious an exercise for this study. But for our purposes we must at least register Wordsworth's insistence—drawn from the experience he so marvellously evokes—that nature meets the child in many guises and moods. The opening books of *The Prelude* form an extended argument in which he explores and illustrates these complex ways in which nature influences the child's spirit. Nature may touch the child's life by way of 'fearless visitings'. Or those visitations may be 'with soft alarm'. But there will also be 'severer interventions'—we recall Wordsworth's terrified recollection of a dark mountain peak appearing to loom threateningly over him as he rowed home at dusk across Lake Windermere. The child nourished by nature is, in a word, 'fostered alike by beauty and by fear'. Nature, for the greatest chronicler of out-of-doors childhood, was more than the dancing daffodils about which he wrote one of his slighter poems.

The child—free to wander the countryside as Wordsworth was—is enriched by nature. The corollary, supported by some at least of our memoirs, is that the child's spirit languishes from lack of nourishment when he or she grows up in a city, especially when home is a crowded slum and polluted air blocks out the sun. But we must avoid over-simplification. We cannot accept that the fifty percent of the world's population, who—so we are told—now live in cities, are condemned to spiritual poverty. And as we have already seen, some of our writers, born and brought up in the slums, remember how their deprived childhoods were touched by the transcendent.

There are further grounds for guarding against too sharp a distinction between rural life and urban life—the former ideal for the child's spiritual development, the latter fatal for it. The Romantic Movement has long passed but many memories—and many memoirs—of childhood are still bathed in its light. We have to wonder how far some recollections of Arcadian childhoods are shaped by the continuing influence of unexamined romantic assumptions. Do some writers describe their childhood the way they do because, with Wordsworth at their shoulder—albeit a caricature of the author of *The Prelude*—they think that that is how childhood is supposed to be remembered? We read their idyllic recollections and we wonder whether the reality was quite as they recall it.

We must hold in mind too that, for most of humanity and for most of history, living close to nature has meant living close to destitution. A subsistence farmer in sub-Saharan Africa lives a precarious and wholly unromantic life. Of course we must guard against supposing that the children of such poor places necessarily suffer spiritually. Those who know them well, such as the one to whom this book is dedicated, will warn us against any such conclusion. Nevertheless too much talk of 'clouds of glory' will certainly occlude our perception of children who do not know when next they are going to be fed. We must have in mind as well that in developed countries too, until relatively recently, life used to be just as hard and uncertain for most rural children, as the memoirs some of them later write testify.

Children do not delight in nature when they are hungry. Furthermore for a sensitive child joy in nature can be tempered by awareness of nature's apparent cruelty. Jill Ker Conway, born in 1934 and a future Visiting Professor at the Massachusetts Institute of Technology, was raised in near-total isolation on a family-owned tract of land in the Australian outback. She lived a lonely life, and grew up with no playmates except for her brothers. Nature, above all its immense unpopulated empty spaces, was certainly formative for her.

'The silence was so profound that it pressed upon the eardrums...Here, pressed into the earth by the weight of that enormous sky, there is real peace. To those who know it, the annihilation of the self, subsumed into the vast emptiness of nature, is akin to a religious experience. We children grew up to know it and seek it as our father before us. What was social and sensory deprivation for the stranger was the earth and sky that made us what we were' (Conway, 1998, 25).

But the environment that shapes her is the stage for much that is cruel and meaningless. She asks her father why God should allow the crows to pick out the eyes of newborn lambs. Her father tells her sadly that he does not know (42).

Geoffrey Dennis remembers the same horror and bewilderment when he comes across an illustration in a school text-book.

'In pictures you saw it. Hideous anguish on baboon's face in my Natural History as leopard's paw comes down to claw his head off; grotesque terrible unmerited anguish lined in his howling face' (Dennis, 1957, 105).

In turning now to happier memories of childhood days spent out-of-doors, we do not forget how hostile an environment the natural world has proved for many children. Nor do we ignore such children as Jill Conway and Geoffrey Dennis who witness nature 'red in tooth and claw' and do not like what they see.

'The trees were my friends'

Cruel as nature can be, many of our writers rejoiced in it when they were young.

On spring mornings Robin Fedden stood in a Normandy garden 'tranced by the birds' chorus'. This experience of sudden enchantment, of being 'tranced' as he calls it, frequently overtakes him.

> 'Once almost anything would work the spell: a fern, a snail shell, the gloss of new chestnuts or a glow-worm in the palm of my hand as I went up to bed' (Fedden, 1964, 29).

Now that they are older our writers try to find some explanation of why the natural world meant so much to them. The novelist Rosemary Sutcliff makes the point that small children are nearer to nature for the simple reason that they are closer to the ground. But spiritually their proximity is closer still. Children are near 'in the sense of kinship'—they are near relatives of nature. Rosemary Sutcliffe describes how the child she was discovered downland turf for the first time.

> 'Above all, I soaked in the "feel" of the downs, the warm sense of the ground itself holding one up; a sureness, a steadfastness; and the sense that one gets in down country of kinship with a land that has been mixed up with the life of men since it and men began' (Sutcliff, 1984, 36-37).

Our writers recognise that at the heart of their encounters with living things was a sense of relationship. That intimacy with nature is voiced in the relational vocabulary they use, in their talk of 'friendship', 'kinship', 'companionship', and the like. We underline what Jill Ker Conway says about the empty landscape that surrounded her and her friends, how they came 'to know it and seek it as our father'. As children, they did not speak of that relationship, but the fact that it was beyond their power to articulate did not make it any less real.

Striking testimony to the spiritual connectedness between child and nature comes from different cultures. Powerful voices from the East speak of it.

Here we turn once more to Rabindranath Tagore, a towering figure warranting far fuller consideration than we can pay him in these pages. A close affinity with the natural order is felt throughout Tagore's many autobiographical writings:

> 'The sky seemed to bring to me the call of a personal companionship, and all my heart—my whole body in fact—used to drink in at a draught the overflowing light and peace of those silent hours…This world was living to me, intimately close to my life, permeated by a subtle touch of kinship' (Tagore, 1931, 99).

To be sure, Tagore did not have to labour on the land as most Bengali children did—and still do. His was an aristocratic land-owning family. But Tagore believed that the kinship with nature he knew as a child was the birthright of all children, rich or poor. Tagore's first love was for the trees and it comes as no surprise that in 'the poet's school' he later founded children gathered beneath the trees—and occasionally *in* the trees—for their lessons. He speaks of 'the great brotherhood of trees' and of 'the invitation of the forest'.

> 'As a boy of ten I stood alone on the Himalayas under the shade of great deodars, awed by the dignity of life's first-born aristocracy, by a fortitude that was terrible as well as courteous' (Tagore, cited in Tagore and Elmhirst, 1961, 51).

Again he writes:

> 'I remember, when I was a child, that a row of coconut trees by our garden wall, with their branches beckoning the rising sun on the horizon, gave a companionship as living as I was myself' (Tagore, 1926, 8).

Tagore is far from alone in delighting in trees. Elisaveta Fen grew up in Russia, later living in London where she trained and worked as a child psychotherapist. Fen understood children, among them the child she herself once was. For her, 'everything in nature seemed imbued with friendliness', but, as for Tagore, her best friends were the trees. As a child, she loved especially a group of rowan trees on her father's estate. 'I imagined that they were feeling rather lonely, and as their grey-green, lacy leaves always rustled on my approach, I liked to think that they were greeting me'. She falls into a conversation with them. 'The trees were my friends; each had a voice of its own: the birch had a light, intimate whisper, the aspen, a nervous, fluttering voice, the oak, a full steady murmur' (Fen, 1961, 137-138). She apologises to a tree when she breaks off one of its branches. During the evening before she leaves for school, she slips into the orchard and says goodbye to the trees one by one (284-285).

Marrie Walsh was an Irish country child. Sometimes her father would have to fell a tree on their farm. This is a distressing time for Marrie and her siblings. 'We would tell the tree the reason for cutting it down. Then we would run round the other trees and tell them not to cry' (Walsh, 2010, 8).

The poet Richard Church is another who exults in the trees. He recalls running between them in the wind. He remembers the trees, 'making me crazed so that I would attempt to imitate their huge gestures, flinging up my arms as I ran, and uttering incoherent noises in my efforts to capture their rhythm and their almost monstrous beauty' (Church, 1955, 192-194).

For the American theologian Frederick Buechner, his childhood was Eden. 'I had dominion over all the earth and over every living thing that moves upon the earth'—not least the trees. 'I knew trees before I knew what a tree was' (Buechner, 1982, 12). Kirsty (R. G. Graham) grew up in the late Victorian period in Berwick-on-Tweed, a town straddling the border between England and Scotland. Kirsty and her friends walk through the trees and by the river. Both trees and river are the children's companions. 'The first scattered trees walked arm-in-arm with them...They were small sisters to the river' (Graham, 1961, 52-53).

Looking back, Kirsty sees the natural order as attuned to the seasonal rhythms of human life.

'The river moved up the autumn banks like a vast poem of fulfilment for the young; then ebbed seaward with a soothing *nunc dimittis* for the old. To everyone his time, his season, his ending, in an order none questioned' (Graham, 1961, 82).

We notice how Kirsty, now an adult writer, slips naturally into the liturgical and scriptural language she will have learned as a child. We shall turn later to the importance of such a mother tongue for our spiritual flourishing.

'One with it in a world of wings'

In some of our memoirs, the recalled relationship is closer still. In a manner that, as an adult, I find hard to comprehend but which I have no grounds to dismiss, the child becomes one in spirit with the natural order.

Elisaveta Fen's sister cries, 'Look at the sky!'

'I turned. The windows were ablaze with sunset, and at once I was ravished, as the unearthly light poured into me through my eyes, and I poured myself into it, becoming one with it for a few incredible moments' (Fen, 1961, 31-32).

Richard Hillyer, who grew up in rural poverty at the beginning of the twentieth century, is one with the birds he watches.

'It might be no more than a bird preening itself on some isolated twig that stood out above the hedgerow against a bright sky; and all at once I would be at one with it in a world of wings, and great spaces, and freedom, and pulsing delight' (Hillyer, 1967, 140).

Elizabeth Hamilton insists that her relationship with the creatures that share her world was 'more than an affinity'. It was 'identification'. 'There were moments when I myself was the heron spreading its vast umbrella wings; the blunt-footed caterpillar curling round a raspberry cane; the horse stamping in the loose box' (Hamilton, 1963, 37). The Bloomsbury child Angelica Garnett even identifies with the insects in her garden. 'I was each ant, each beetle; I knew what it was to have six legs and swivel eyes, to hesitate, searching for information with trembling antennae, suspicious and fearful' (Garnett, 1984, 44).

This sense of something more than kinship is felt by children of all cultures. In his quaint English—an idiom he deliberately cultivated—the Japanese writer Yoshio Markino recalls that as a child:

'I was always a friend to the Nature. If I went out to the open field I enjoyed to breathe the fresh air first, then those singing birds seemed as if they were calling me. Even branches of the tree looked as if they were beckoning me. And I went deeply into the Nature as if I were one of them. When I leaned against a tree I felt I was a tree, and when I watched a bird I felt I was a bird too. Sometimes I was a light butterfly flying over the meadow flowers. Sometimes I was a cricket singing in the bushes. I quite remember I spent a whole morning watching the twinkling stream of the crystal-like water of the River Yada, and my soul was flowing in it. I picked up a snow-white blossom of Sagi-So to smell its scent and I forgot whether I was the flower or that little flower in my own hands was myself' (Markino, 1912, 134).

Here are adults claiming that their relationship with nature as children amounted at times to a symbiosis, to a fusion of their own life with that of the living things in which they delighted. 'I myself was the heron,' says Elizabeth Hamilton (Hamilton, 1963, 37).

It is an aspect of a child's spirituality that is little noticed or appreciated and today, in a culture that keeps children indoors, rarely promoted. These claims to a oneness with nature are not to be dismissed as far-fetched or to be taken as the imposition of alien adult categories on the child's perceptions. Some children at least seem to be aware of nature in ways which most of us as adults have lost. And however studiously 'green' we are in our world-view, it is a loss we must lament.

'Happiness, self-kindling as the lark's'

The child's relationship with nature can be ecstatic. Ida Gandy grew up in the rectory of a remote windswept Wiltshire parish. Like the young Shelley, rejoicing in the wild west wind, she loved an autumn day,

> 'when a big wind was let loose in the world. Then indeed we became, more than at any time, a part of the wildness and freedom, as much in the power of the wind as the hurrying host of leaves torn from the beechwoods, as the thistledown sailing shoulder-high, or the torn clouds' (Gandy, 1929, 91-92).

She becomes part of all that delights her. Her ecstasy in the wind is echoed by Eleanor ('Milly') Acland who cries, 'I am the wind. I *am* the wind' (Acland, 1935, 133). Later we shall see in Anne Treneer's *Schoolhouse in the Wind*, one of our great Cornish autobiographies of childhood, how such abandonment to the wind can be understood in Biblical terms, as a Pentecostal experience of the Holy Spirit.

When Frank Kendon, growing up in Kent, explored the wood above the school which was his home, 'the whole of the wood was one creature, and that one spoke somehow to my spirit' (Kendon, 1950, 16).

> 'The spring came from the earth into us, the riot of the summer also troubled our blood, and in all we were the creatures' brothers. We, too, were straws in the long currents of life, and our happiness was as self-kindling as the lark's and, like the lark, we hardly knew we sang' (149-150).

For one child at least, his joy in nature is almost too much for him. In Serghei Aksakoff's *Years of Childhood* we meet a child so transported by delight at the coming of spring that his mother fears for his mental balance. The little boy follows every stage of the advancing spring. 'How many sensations for me! How I shouted for joy!' He is moved to ecstasy by the coming of the birds. 'I seemed, and could not but seem, a crazy half-witted creature: my eyes were wild, I could see nothing and heard not a word of what was said to me'. He is intoxicated by all that is coming to new birth in the awakening countryside—though he is fearful too. Now that the jackdaws are sitting on their nests, he is terrified that the circling kite might swoop down and seize the hen's tiny chicks.

The season of spring, with its myriad signs of new life, is also the season of Easter and young Serghei enters into the celebration of the festival with the same exultant abandonment with which he greets nature's renewal. But one Easter of his childhood is clouded by tragedy. The local miller is drowned in a river in spate. The boy is apprehensive that such a catastrophe could overtake any of them at any moment. Yet the sense of new life, with which the season abounds, proves stronger than the experience of death. By juxtaposing his account of the miller's death with that of nature's death and resurrection, Aksakoff suggests that, even as a child, he was aware of an organic correlation between the two notwithstanding his inability as a child to find words for it.

As Serghei Aksakoff recalls his first spring in the country, the resonances with Wordsworth are strong. For Wordsworth, the child's intimacy with nature, though beyond recovery, bestows a lifelong blessing. 'The thought of our past years,' he writes, 'in me doth breed perpetual benediction' (*Ode on the Intimations of Immortality from Recollections of Early Childhood*). Aksakoff concludes, 'But this I know, that the thought of that time has been, throughout my whole life, a source of quiet happiness in my heart' (Aksakoff. 1923, 287-307).

Colin Middleton Murry is another who interprets his relationship with nature as a child in Wordsworthian terms.

'I became a thorough-going pantheist without realising it. When, years later, I came across the line in *Tintern Abbey*: "Nature then to me was All in All", I knew at once what Wordsworth meant. I recognized myself. In the Larling woods, on the heaths, among the fields and fens, I found peace. And something more than peace. I found an element, a spirit, that was not indifferent to me; did not reject me...I watched the birds like a spy until I found their hidden nests, but felt no urge to take their eggs. What I collected was private knowledge—incidents that were known to myself alone—yet all the while I was conscious of that incommunicable sense of having been there before, of rediscovering things already known'.

The young Colin was a shy lonely child and not invariably happy. As we saw, he was cruelly bullied at school. But nature drew him to herself.

'Out of doors, beneath those limitless Norfolk skies, I needed no one, became part of what I was among. Even when unhappiness seemed all but insupportable and the tears would not stop, there was always a time when my attention was drawn outside myself to some small wonder of the world without' (Murry, 1975, 59).

Murry describes how much later—in his mid-teens and grieving deeply the sudden death of a close friend—he was alone fishing when he was overwhelmed by a profound sense that he was not alone. 'It was just an absolute *awareness*,' he tells us. To deny the subjective truth of such an experience, he comments, 'would be tantamount to the denial of my own human existence' (198).

Nature and naturalists

As a boy, the naturalist W. H. Hudson roamed the vast Argentine pampas. His *Far Away and Long Ago* is one of the classical accounts of childhood and his chapter (xvii) entitled 'A Boy's Animism' is one of our most important sources. Here Hudson analyses his intense awareness of the natural world and his relationship with it. He speaks of 'the sense and apprehension of an intelligence like our own but more powerful in all visible things'. Hudson argues that 'this sense of the supernatural in natural things' remains acute among those 'born and bred amidst rural surroundings', but in towns and crowded places it withers and dies. Hudson confesses, 'I never spoke of these feelings to others'. Many other adults in recalling the 'unattended moments' of their childhood say much the same. Hudson claims that this 'faculty or instinct'—akin, he believes, to the animism (as he saw it) of Traherne and the pantheism of Wordsworth—is 'essentially religious in character', although he fears that the narrowly orthodox will perceive such a disposition as 'a temptation of the evil one'.

As a boy Hudson believed implicitly in what he had been taught about 'the Supreme Being'. 'But apart from the fact that the powers above would save me in the end from extinction,' he writes, 'which was a great consolation, these teachings did not touch my heart as it was touched and thrilled by something nearer, more intimate, in nature.' Formal religion fails him for it does not acknowledge and endorse all that so delights him.

Hudson does however give one example of someone who showed that it was possible to reconcile 'faith in revealed religion with...animistic emotion'. He remembers hearing of a perfectly orthodox Christian believer, the owner of a grand estate, who, before retiring each night, would walk through his park, whispering good-night to his trees one-by-one (Hudson, 1931, 224-235).

Richard Jefferies, like W. H. Hudson, was a naturalist. His *Bevis* is a fictional account of a boy growing up on a Wiltshire farm, but closely based on his own childhood. Like Hudson's great work, it records a childhood lived out in the borderland between this world and another.

Bevis and his friend Mark are attentive children.

'They listened: the wood was still; so still they could hear a moth or a chafer entangled in the leaves of the oak overhead, and trying to get out...The long, long summer days seemed to dispose the mind to something unusual. Out of such an expanse of light, when the earth is tangibly in the midst of a vast illumined space, what may not come?—Perhaps something more than is common to the senses' (Jefferies, 1932, 76).

The boys chase each other in and out of the sycamore trees.

'The sunlight poured upon them, and the light air came along; they bathed in air and sun-beam, and gathered years of health like flowers from the field'.

Their world was suffused in light. 'The swallows flew in light, the fish swam in light, the trees stood in light'. 'Magic,' said Bevis. 'It's magic' (126).

Bevis looks up to the night sky. 'At that first sight of Orion's shoulder Bevis always felt stronger, as if a breath of the mighty hunter had come down and entered into him' (351). 'As he listened and watched the swallows he thought, or rather felt—for he did not think from step to step upwards to a conclusion—he felt that all the power of a bird's wing is in its tip' (465).

'The power of a bird's wing is in its tip.' It is an astonishing insight. Richard Jefferies is careful here to distinguish the child's immediate intense experience—this is what the child *felt*—from the adult's subsequent account of that experience. Only the child could sense what he did; only the grown-up can say what it was he sensed. Whatever one later makes of it and however one describes it, the perception, Jefferies insists, remains the child's.

Empathy with animals

As we have seen, a strong empathy exists between children and animals, even if not all children identify with the insects they meet quite as intimately as Angelica Garnett who knew what it was to have six legs and swivel eyes. We like to think that all children love animals, at least animals that are safe enough and small enough to play with. But the evidence from our memoirs is that the child's relationship with living creatures is rather more complicated and that it is not always joyful or benign. On the one hand a child will often feel keenly for an animal in pain; on the other hand a child—sometimes the same child—will find pleasure in causing an animal to suffer.

A child's sympathy for a creature that is suffering, or that seems to be suffering, or that has died, can be seen as an aspect of the 'relational consciousness' which David Hay and Rebecca Nye see as the heart of a child's spirituality. A few examples from many that could be cited must suffice.

Elisaveta Fen tells us how her heart burned as a child when she came upon the common sight of 'a peasant pony desperately straining its tin neck, its small hoofs kneading the ground at an ever-increasing speed, in an effort to pull an overloaded cart out of a muddy patch'. For this questioning child, the plight of 'the much maltreated peasant ponies of Russia' posed a theological problem. 'Surely they were innocent, and in all fairness deserved to go to paradise' (Fen, 1961, 165-166).

R. G. Graham (Kirsty) remembers the sorrow, as she perceived it, of the corncrake:

'The evening, a minute ago folded serenely around (Kirsty) like a luminous shawl, had been torn, and an inner aching united her to this sound...In rather a whimper she announced, "I don't like yon bird. It's greeting"' (Graham, 1961, 40).

'Greeting' is a Tyneside expression for crying.

Bryan Magee, who grew up between the wars in London's East End, when much traffic was still horse-drawn, felt for the suffering of the horses. 'Essentially, the feeling was one of identification: when I looked at a horse it was as if I *was* the horse; and if I saw it being ill-treated the inner painfulness of that to me was nigh unbearable' (Magee, 2003, 234).

The family of the Danish composer Carl Nielsen had a horse named Samson. The boy Carl is devastated when it has to be put down.

'We felt it doubly pitiful because we could see that Samson had no suspicion that his time had come. The whole world was wonderfully beautiful: the birds were singing in the distance; the swallows that had built their nests on the walls flitted happily to and fro, and their young screamed for joy in the nests each time they were fed. My brother and I went sadly into a shed and sat a while on some planks. A quarter of an hour passed and we heard a gunshot' (Nielsen, 1953, 32-33).

Similarly, James Kirkup records how intensely he pitied a horse that had to be shot after it had run away with a cart and had careered over, breaking its legs (*Kirkup*, 1957, 115-116).

Cruelty to animals.

In contrast to such instances of children's compassion for suffering creatures, there are, alas, examples of just how cruel to animals the child can be. Bryan Magee may have loved horses, but he makes his tortoise Joey pay for not responding to him, by 'throwing him up high in the air and letting him smash down on the concrete' (Magee, 2003, 279).

Tsewang Pemba, looking back on his Tibetan childhood, admits that he and his friends were very cruel to animals.

'The things we did to them would not make good reading to say the least; we were little brutes...I hope that people will not think that Tibetan boys are sweet cherubic creatures taking flowers and sundry offerings to the local monastery' (Pemba, 1957, 21).

Some of our writers claim that, even as children, they recognised that their unkindness to animals was wrong. The Indian child, Mulk Raj Anand, drops a kitten in a well. 'I did not realise the horror of my deed at the time...' he writes. 'I could hear God, with many voices, whistling in the dark of my head, his big bearded face craning over me and saying, "You will see how I shall punish you for this"' (Anand, 2005, 37-38).

The Japanese boy, Yoshio Markino, makes a trap to catch sparrows, but the spring is too strong and he kills one.

'He was bleeding vermilion red. I felt so sad for the poor bird. I buried him in my garden, and made a grave with this inscription: "Here lies a poor unlucky sparrow who so innocently was trapped by a wicked human being. I sincerely repent"' (Markino, 1912, 37).

Frank Kendon, growing up in Kent, becomes aware of 'the "brotherhood" of all living creatures to which he belongs'. This kinship is brought home to him by the death of a wren, killed by a stone one of the village boys throws. He realises that the creatures are 'dreadfully equal with us'. The killing of the bird, in which he tacitly complies, proves to be a decisive moment in his spiritual formation.

'Through all those long days of our first decade beauty had shone about us and love had poured itself into us, largely unknown to us because we had never known the absence of these things. The spirit had silently been preparing that we might bear sorrows, and that very moment when we looked at the dead wren (though there were others no doubt, less memorable), becomes the moment of initiation' (Kendon, 1950, 152-154).

Similarly John Raynor, as he looks back, recognises the moral and spiritual significance of a cruel act he perpetrated as a boy. He had always loved butterflies, but one day he wantonly kills one. 'I knew that I was never really innocent; I was always fighting something; whereas the butterfly, of its nature, was truly innocent.' To become aware of his own capacity for cruelty was, he adds, to feel the burden of 'original sin' (Raynor, 1973, 124).

'Look at the birds of the air'

We shall return to children's experiences of nature in our next chapter when we hear memories of moments of ecstatic awareness—'peak experiences', as they have been called—for which the world of nature was often the setting. But first we pause to ask what we learn about our own discipleship from the child's evident affinity with nature and what that affinity calls for in the spiritual education of children.

Amongst much else that it demands of us, the command to become a child requires us to step out of doors. But more of us is being asked than we get out into the fresh air. The keynote of a childhood spent close to nature, so our memoirs have taught us, is kinship. To be a child is to be attuned to nature and to turn and become a child is to recover that sense of kinship. Rather more is required of us than a commitment to our environment and to its protection and preservation, imperative as that requirement is. The consciousness of the child I must recover is the 'relational consciousness' of the child who identifies with living things.

The most familiar exemplar in the Christian tradition of an adult indwelled by the spirit of the child at one with nature is St Francis. Francis obeyed Christ's injunction 'Look at the birds of the air'. The Greek behind Jesus's familiar words means 'Look *carefully* at the birds'. The command amounts to a bidding to be open to a relationship. The same applies to Christ's call to consider 'the lilies of the field'. More is being asked of us than that we all become 'twitchers' or expert botanists, although clearly we are not going to learn much from birds and wild flowers unless we sometimes stop what we foolishly suppose could be more important and go out and look at them.

Nature and Nurture

Few grown-ups in the part the world where I write claim a 'kinship with nature', however many television programmes about wild-life they watch or however green their politics. Fewer still would claim to be one with nature. A constituent element of a child's spirituality has been all but extinguished in us. What we have lost is not some 'childish thing' rightly put away. We have taken leave of something vital to our humanity. The loss can be attributed to many causes, but primarily to the drift from a rural culture to an urban culture—a drift that has taken place irrespective of whether home is in a city or in the country. One fears that today country children in the so-called 'developed world' are as much wedded to their indoor gizmos, their video games and the rest, as are city children.

Most of the memories quoted in this chapter of growing-up close to nature are recollections of childhoods of a generation or more ago. When we read these memories—when we register just how richly children were once nourished by their nearness to living things—we are bound to recognise the contrasting spiritual impoverishment of our own children whose experience of the natural world is so meagre.

Bertram Smith remembers the freedom of his Scottish childhood. He writes of a day out of doors, 'We had run wild without stint or let or hindrance' (Bertram Smith, 1920, 33). Smith called his memoir *Running Wild*. How many accounts of contemporary childhoods, we wonder, could have that title?

Today's 'indoor children' suffer from what has been described as a 'nature deficit disorder'. As Richard Louv has argued in his seminal *Last Child in the Woods* (Louv, 2008), sensationalist media coverage, paranoid parents, and the lure of the screen have exiled children from what could be called their natural habitat. The task of spiritual education and Christian nurture is to give back to children some sense of their extended family and their true home.

We turn again to Tagore. Tagore believed that we find our meaning and fulfilment relationally; in our relationships one with another, to be sure, but fundamentally in our kinship with all that is. He taught that we must be liberated from the bounds of individual separateness and so discover a wholeness larger than our personal well-being. That wholeness is ultimately realised in our union with the eternal Divine Spirit—with the one whom many call God.

Tagore believed that growing children must be in vital contact with the world of nature. To be in touch with nature is to relate to the One nature betokens. Tagore rejects the assumption that nature is there merely to meet our needs. We find God, we find one another, and we find ourselves, by relinquishing the central role we have assigned ourselves in the scheme of things and by recovering our true relationship with the natural order.

Tagore feared that traditional forms of education serve only to disconnect and to disenchant. For example, the more facts drummed into a child about trees, the less able he or she is to see the tree outside the classroom window. Tagore relates how a successful headmaster once visited the school he, Tagore, had founded. The headmaster is appalled to see a child sitting reading a book in the fork of a tree. Tagore explains to his shocked visitor why that child's choice where to sit does not trouble him. 'Childhood is the only period of life when a civilized man can exercise his choice between a tree and a chair. Why deprive a child of that privilege because I, as a grown-man, am barred from it?' (Tagore and Elmhirst, 1961, 117-119)

There has been much talk about trees in this chapter. Tagore believed that it is a vital part of education to encourage children to love trees simply because they are lovable as it is to teach them the scientific reasons why trees are necessary for our survival. There are additional compelling scriptural reasons for making much of trees in any curriculum that claims a Christian framework, for the Bible claims that, as we fell because of a tree, so we are saved because of a tree. But such imagery will begin to make sense only as we first relate to real trees as many of the children we have met in this chapter did.

Spiritual education and Christian nurture—walking with children along the way of Jesus—is thus bound to be counter-cultural. Its task is to throw open windows to the wider world and to our family of living things that inhabits it. A periodic relocation of our ministry to children, usually an indoor activity, will be needed. The yew tree in the churchyard has waited for a thousand years for children to gather beneath its branches. The time has come to reward its patience.

CHAPTER 6

'pRINCe of The Apple TOWNS'

'And honoured among wagons I was prince of the apple towns.'
The thrilling words are from Dylan Thomas's *Fern Hill*, a poem
evoking the intensity, the immediacy, and the evanescence of a
child's life. Here he captures one exultant moment from his childhood
when, at the end of an autumn day harvesting an orchard, he rides back to
the farm in a horse-drawn wagon, enthroned on apples.

I turn in this chapter to such experiences, which many have known
but of which few speak. In a book of particular interest to us, for it too
draws on published autobiographies, Michael Paffard has described such
moments as 'so out of the ordinary as to seem to belong to a dimension
other than the quotidian, to be epiphanies of another order of reality'
(Paffard, 1976, 8).

Such 'unattended moments'—the turn of phrase is from T. S. Eliot's
Four Quartets—have become the subject of much interest over the last
fifty years. They were investigated by the psychologist Abraham Maslow
in his seminal study *Religions, Values, and Peak Experiences* (Maslow, 1994).
Edward Robinson reflected on experiences of this kind in two brief but
fascinating books, both published by Religious Experience Research Unit,
as it was then called, (*Original Vision*, 1977, and *Living the Questions*, 1978).
As we mentioned earlier, the Religious Experience Research Centre, as it is
has been renamed, retains an extensive archive of these recalled memories
of childhood's 'peak experiences'.

We begin with a memory that was of extraordinary importance to the
one who shares it with us.

Virginia Woolf tells us that two very early recollections compete for
the status of her first memory. Of one of these she says, 'It is the most
important of all my memories.' She does not tell us how old she was, but
certainly it is a memory from early infancy. The child—who one day will
write *The Waves*—is lying in bed in the nursery at St Ives, half asleep, half

awake. She hears the rhythmic breaking of the waves on the beach and watches the light flooding into the room as the wind lifts the blind. Her memory is of 'hearing this splash and seeing this light, and feeling it is almost impossible that I should be here, of feeling the purest ecstasy I can conceive'. Virginia Woolf says of this intense experience: 'If life has a base that it stands upon, if it is a bowl that one fills and fills and fills—then my bowl without a doubt stands upon this memory' (Virginia Woolf, 1989, 72-73). Here is evidence that these rapturous moments can be experienced as early in life as memory can recall. Indeed we are bound to wonder whether such experiences were ours even before memory began keeping records.

I turn to Paul Ashton who, as we saw, grew up in a strict Plymouth Brethren household. Ashton recalls three experiences in his childhood of what he describes as 'visionary states'. As a five-year-old, he tells us, three angels appeared to him in his school playground. In later years Ashton will realise that in fact these angels were three chefs, wearing their tall white hats, leaning out of a window of Westminster College which abutted his school. But in his memory they remain for him angels. Their status as such is uncompromised and the ecstatic experience of their visitation undiminished by the rational explanation of their identity.

Two years later he was taken by his grandfather to the banks of the Thames opposite Battersea Power Station. The Thames was in flood— it was January 1953 and that year floodwater had already killed many along England's east coast. Ashton describes how he and his grandfather suddenly find themselves up to their knees in water, so swiftly is the river rising. Ashton recalls 'an ecstasy of power and mingled terror and elation.'

'What I really wanted to do was to wade right into the river, pick up the power station and shake it as if it were one of those glass domes with a snowstorm inside, and stride along the river stepping over the bridges one by one, and laughing. I wanted to drink the river and have it forever inside me and flowing through me' (Ashton, 2013, 60-62).

Ashton remembers a third 'mystical experience'. He is on a camping holiday with his 'Crusader' Bible class on the Isle of Wight. One of his chores is to burn the rubbish. The bonfire, on which the leftovers from the day's meals are burning, suddenly kindles in the boy an awareness of some 'transcendent other'. Ashton's extended description of this experience, his meticulous observation of the fire and of the vision that overtakes him, is one of the most powerful records of such a 'peak experience' that we have encountered in our literature. Alas, it is too long to cite in full, but one or two features of young Paul Ashton's experience need to be registered.

It is an experience of boundless joy. The child notices the eggshells crackling in the flames. 'They seemed to have been created by a divine hand...They all leaned on each other in a way that was perfect, inevitable and full of joy, and I began to feel that joy go through me.' Furthermore, he recognises that what he witnesses is in some sense a disclosure. He sees the burning onion leaves, potato peelings and carrot tops as living beings—'all of them ecstatically happy in their existence and its transformation, and celebrating the perfect oneness of their material and their spiritual beings which they had always known about *and which they were now teaching me*'.

I emphasise those last words to register that the vision of the transcendent, if such it was, directly addresses the one who witnesses it and imparts lessons to be learned. Long ago among the Lakes the child Wordsworth had similarly experienced such overwhelming moments as admonitory and didactic.

What Paul sees is close to a theophany.

'I realised with intense pleasure that I was seeing something like the vision the prophet Ezekiel saw...I was overjoyed that a similar crystalline vision had been vouchsafed to me too. I knew immediately that without leaving the physical world I was in the divine presence, and I had a small intimation of why the seraphim and cherubim...do nothing but gaze on God and praise him' (117-119).

Paul Ashton adds that he knew that for the rest of his life he would draw strength and comfort from this vision. The importance for us of what this young boy experienced—he was thirteen at the time—is not that it proved formative for his religious faith. Indeed the rest of Ashton's memoir maps what he describes as his 'zigzag path to unbelief'. What strikes us is that the child sensed his experience as *revelatory*. We cannot, with any kind of philosophical integrity, close our minds to the possibility, that such real experiences, however else they may be explained, can be experiences of the Real.

A further point of interest is the language Paul uses to describe this experience. That experience, as he recalls it, owed nothing to the religion of his Brethren assembly. The Brethren would have been appalled by a child of their number claiming to have met God in a bonfire. Nor would his experience have been accommodated by the evangelicalism of the Crusaders, a movement with which the present writer was associated for many years. The theophany granted to this child, if it was that, was a vertical intervention into the horizontal, a breaking in on the sober confessional pietism of his assembly and his Bible class. And yet, and yet, he uses Biblical language to account for what took place. He 'spoke Christian'. In later chapters I shall underline the evidence from our memoirs of the necessity of a fitting language if the spiritual is to be articulated—though to be sure the Spirit is famous for speaking in many tongues.

Mary Austin writes in the third person of the child she was. She was five or six and by herself on the brow of a hill. (Something has already been said about the mistaken prudence that forbids today's child to be alone on the brow of a hill.)

> 'Quite suddenly, after a moment of quietness there, earth and sky and tree and wind-blown grass and the child in the midst of them came alive together with a pulsing light of consciousness. There was a wild foxglove at the child's feet and a bee dozing about it.'

The adult Mary Austin adds, 'To this day I can recall the swift inclusive awareness of each for the whole—I in them and they in me and all of us enclosed in a warm lucent bubble of livingness' (Austin, 1931, cited in Paffard, 1976, 17).

The experience of such moments is of life at a new level. Francesca Allinson, born into Bloomsbury's outer circle, hated 'the chasm that deepened more and more between the day's reality and (her) own'. She tries and fails to reconcile these two orders of existence. She looks into a mirror and is 'rapt away' by what she sees. The reflection transfigures the ordinary—an old hat, a match-box, a lamp, a chair. The worlds either side of the mirror correspond to the duality of her experience.

'On the one side were ranged the wearing of galoshes, the learning of arithmetic, and the routine of pushing one's chair into the table after meals...; on the other side was I, the I that played ecstatic games, had seen snow lie for a few magical hours on London roofs, and that sat blissfully in the firelight beside my mother while she told me stories...And then one day my own manicure set tripped up all my objections to it, by catching a sparkle on its scissors that made spring shout and clamour' (Allinson, 1937, 103).

The poet Richard Church's serious short-sightedness was not diagnosed until he was seven. When he finally put on the glasses belatedly prescribed for him, he saw the world as for the first time. His account of 'this blazing and trumpeting invasion' has echoes of Traherne's 'the corn stood orient and immortal wheat'. When he looked up into the 'traffic of the night sky', it was, he tells us, 'a revelation to my newly educated eyes'. 'I floated away, and might have disappeared into space had not a cry recalled me' (Church, 1955, 69-70).

Church suggests that such an experience constitutes some kind of disclosure. That is what he senses when he is given a set of water-colours. These throw him into 'ecstasies of happiness and *discovery*, (in the mystic's sense of that word)' (Church, 1955, 128). (The italics are the author's.)

The child ascending

Some of the extraordinary experiences Richard Church recalls suggest a mystical awareness which we might suppose is granted only to those far advanced on the spiritual path. After a period of illness—he must have been nine or ten at the time—he is sent to a sanatorium on the Kent coast to recuperate. One morning, as he is about to go downstairs to breakfast, he experiences a sense of levitation.

'On that frosty morning, between getting up and going down to breakfast, in an antiseptic, varnished institution where the inmates and staff were so dehumanised that they were little more than parts of the mechanism of the place, leaving me in a murmurous solitude, day after day bemused and lonely, elated by the very dreariness of things, there I stood transfigured, with that astounding companion, the Jesus whom I had fashioned from my reading in the Bible; there I stood and turned to him with an eagerness to impart my finding, to share the significance, the richness of it' (Church, 1955, 159).

'I soared higher, half way to the ceiling', he tells us.

'Again and again, during moments of isolation, when thought or some imaginative fervour so elevated my spirits that I had to express my worship and devotion to Jesus my Companion, in some instant deed, I practised the now habitual contraction of muscles, the dilution of my blood with a slow indraught of air, and experienced the divine sensation of rising from the ground to command a new dimension'

Richard Church comments,

'These moments are rare, and they are wholly vital. For a flash, the recogniser is a god, who can say 'I am', as Jehovah said in the Old Testament.'

The adult Church reflects that such experiences tell us that both time and space can be overcome and that 'other seemingly stable laws of nature might be questioned...to the advantage of this fettered and hoodwinked spirit'. Church does not reflect, as we are bound to, on the further implication of such a moment, that a child too can ascend Mount Tabor and be blessed there with a mountain-top experience beyond that of even Peter, James and John (Church, 1955, 159-164).

Church is not the only child to experience moments of ecstatic exultation, but what is interesting is that he instinctively uses Christian language to talk about them. He tells us that while copying a Turner print, 'one of those revelations took place, suddenly, while I was plodding away, and a door was flung open in my consciousness, flung open with a bang by the wind that bloweth where it listeth, at no man's bidding' (198).

Of course, it is Church the grown-up speaking when he alludes to St John's account of the activity of the Spirit of God (John 3.8). He is voicing his later awareness of what was going on. The interpretation is the adult's.

But it was the small boy who, in a bleak sanatorium on the Kentish coast, met Jesus on the mountain top and knew that it was he.

Richard Church gives an explicitly Christian account of what happened to him, but his experience of something akin to levitation is not unique to the child of a Christian culture. The Indian boy, Mulk Raj Anand, describes what he felt when on one occasion his father carried him home on his shoulders.

'I suddenly felt lighter than air. I had the sensation that I was floating upwards into the sky. Then the dark whorl of the evening descended upon me and closed my eyes, and I felt as though I were climbing higher and higher as though the light of the spark lit into me by my father's sing-song had lifted me on high with its strange raucous music and transported me to a city beyond the sky '(Anand, 2005, 49).

James Kirkup, the poet, speaks of a similar experience.

'For many weeks I was convinced that I was the Dalai Lama and that Tibetan monks might be calling me any day to take me off to Lhasa. The room, the ceiling, and the floor would slide away gently into nothingness. I would find my gaze fixed on a few square inches of flowered wallpaper which became a pattern of moving faces, all slightly different from one another, that mouthed silent smiles and curses at my dispirited body. Then I would feel myself hovering outside myself and looking down with dispassionate curiosity at the body I had left lying on our old horse-hair sofa' (Kirkup, 1959, 144-145).

Colin Middleton Murry remembers similar ecstatic moments—and 'ecstatic' is the correct word to describe them, for literally it means 'standing outside' oneself.

'Sometimes the sensation was almost physical as when, lying on my back in the long grass and staring up at the clouds drifting overhead, I felt as though they were drawing me after them and I could look

down on myself from far above. At such time the tether that held
me to my six- year-old self was tenuous indeed' (Murry, 1975, 49).

Like Bevis under another night sky, Jill Conway looks up to the stars,
and, like Bevis, is at one with what all she surveys.

'It was enchanting to lie gazing up at the sky and watch the stars
come out, opening up infinite depths in the heavens. These receding
depths seemed to lift you lightly off the earth, and you could not tell
whether the earth had shrunk to your size, or you had marvellously
expanded until you were fused with all that surrounded you' (Conway,
1998, 280-281).

The child is 'lifted lightly off the earth'. Again the sense of ascension is
physical as well as spiritual. (It is this 'defiance of gravity'—in every sense—that
George MacDonald explores in his marvellous fairy tale *The Light Princess*.)

What are we to make of these experiences? A sense of being levitated
is a not uncommon symptom of psychological disturbance. Merchants of
some meditative techniques claim that the experience of levitation may
be enjoyed by the methods they market. A sense of levitation may be
accurately explained as a process in the mind. Whether it is 'all in the mind'
is quite another matter.

Shaped by joy

Elisaveta Fen's childhood was blessed by moments out of time. She
sees a sunset and is one with its light.

'The windows were ablaze with sunset, and at once I was ravished,
as the unearthly light poured into me through my eyes, and I poured
myself into it, becoming one with it for a few incredible moments'
(Fen, 1961, 31-32).

On a long journey with her family, they pause for the horses to drink
at a river. The driver Maxim is whistling a little sadly. The sun is setting

on the water. 'Ravished, entranced, I gazed, listened, inhaled, felt with the whole of my being, wishing it to go on forever, yet hardly able to bear it a moment longer' (56).

On a picnic on a trip to a convent, she wanders deep into the forest.

'A feeling of great joy rose from somewhere inside me. I breathed a deep sigh: laughter was on my lips and tears in my eyes. All this was mine: the trees, the silence, the sunlight...and I belonged to them and nothing could change it! I heard myself saying: "I love you! I love you! I love you! I did not know to whom I was speaking; it did not matter: I knew I was heard"' (253).

We have noted earlier Elisaveta's intense love of the countryside and of living things. At ecstatic moments such as these, when she becomes aware that her love is reciprocated, a relationship is established. We must register what she says: 'I knew I was heard'. Richard Church (once more), crazed by the trees' huge gestures, 'made boastful passes at the universe'—and, he tells us, 'the great elm responded' (Church, 1955, 192). Such testimony carries great weight. Again we stress that it is doctrinaire in the extreme to assert that such real experiences cannot be experience of the Real.

W. H. Hudson, too, is one with the nature he loves at such exalted moments. He recalls how, when riding on the plain, he would sometimes discover a patch of scarlet verbenas. Then, he tells us, 'I would throw myself from my pony with a cry of joy to lie on the turf among them and feast my sight on their brilliant colour' (Hudson, 1931, 227). At other times, he would 'gaze at the sky, peopled with thistle-down until they are to me living things and I, in an ecstasy, am with them, floating in that immense shining void' (294). As with Richard Church and James Kirkup, the child's exultation is accompanied by a sense of being literally 'lifted up'.

Such experiences are formative. The Russian writer Maxim Gorky, who later will claim much of our attention, recalls 'a mild quiet evening, one of those melancholy evenings of Indian summer' when 'everything is hushed and mute; every sound—the stirring of a bird, the rustle of a falling leaf—seems loud and makes one start warily, only to sink once more into the all-embracing silence which fills the heart. Such moments give rise to thoughts which are particularly pure, but fragile and transparent as a spider's web, defying capture in words...*At such moments character is moulded* (Gorky, 1961, 163). My italics draw attention to Gorky's recognition of the central Wordsworthian principle that nature exercises a moral force.

> 'Therefore am I still well pleased to recognise
> In nature and the language of the sense,
> The anchor of my purest thoughts, the nurse,
> The guide, the guardian of my heart, and soul
> Of all my moral being.'
> (*Lines above Tintern Abbey*)

Children are reluctant to talk about these 'peak experiences', as Maslow calls them. So too are adults. They are secrets we keep to ourselves. Here is a profound tragedy, for our reticence is a failure to acknowledge the spiritual bedrock of our common humanity. Our authors speak about such experiences only when they come at last to write about their childhoods. Only then do they disclose these closely guarded secrets. Richard Hillyer, country child, writes:

> 'Once, I remember, as I was coming home over the rise above the village, the houses below, and the familiar fields suddenly became incredibly beautiful. They were no different to what they had been before, and yet they were different. Joy burned in them....Elation rushed up inside me, as if a barrier had suddenly given way before it. Words, half found lines of poetry, blundered about in my mind, striving to shape themselves into some expression of this intense delight; and in the end verses came, poor, broken-backed things, but seeming at the time to be a miracle. This was my own private revelation, nobody before had ever had such thoughts, they belonged to the secret places of the soul, *and were not to be spoken of even to my brother*' (Hillyer, 1966, 102)

My italics emphasise the child's unwillingness, shared by so many who experience these moments of ecstatic illumination, to disclose them to others.

Such experiences cannot be predicted. Richard Hillyer again:

'Those sudden exaltations that exploded around me, out of nowhere, were what I had to hang on to at all costs; and yet I could not hang on to them, for they came and went as they pleased. Sometimes it was a poem, or a piece of prose, that touched off the magic that brought the lift of the heart that was like a fountain breaking into the sunlight. Sometimes just an ordinary thing would suddenly make itself new and marvellous. It might be no more than a bird preening itself on some isolated twig that stood out above the hedgerow against a bright sky; and all at once I would be at one with it in a world of wings, and great spaces, and freedom, and pulsing delight' (Hillyer, 1966, 140).

The experience can be triggered by something itself unremarkable—a twig in a hedgerow—yet it generates, for the little child as for the adult mystic, a sense of oneness with the transcendent. Hillyer describes having to help his father cut the beans, a job that had to be done very early in the morning: 'The starlight and the dawn met together in a luminous haze, filled a charmed time, that lapped the edge of the world's mysteries' (70).

Frank Kendon, too, discovers that the borderland between night and day can also be the frontier between here and beyond. Sometimes he would venture out as early as five in the morning:

'Everywhere there was the sense of a spirit or creature indifferent to human boys, a spirit who had slipped round out of sight by the snowberry hedge only a moment before, and when I followed, had, I felt, just escaped me again by going out to the road under the fir trees...As I walked along the gritty road and turned up under the cedar tree by the chapel, I again felt that mingling of fear and joy which is ecstasy... it was so lovely that it made me afraid...Times there are when a thousand common beauties strike and are one terrible annihilating sweetness together' (Kendon, 1950, 199-202).

As for Wordworth, as for the saints, the child's experience of the transcendent is as fearful as it is joyful.

Rabindranath Tagore is another for whom morning is a time of disclosure.

'The sun was just rising through the leafy tops of those trees. As I continued to gaze, all of a sudden a covering seemed to fall away from my eyes, and I found the world bathed in a wonderful radiance, with waves of beauty and joy swelling on every side. This radiance pierced in a moment through the folds of sadness and despondency which had accumulated over my heart and flooded it with this universal light' (Tagore, 1917, 217).

For the Australian writer D. R. Burns too, one ecstatic moment of childhood was an experience of a flood of light. He embarks with his best friend Lenny—unwashed, 'free as the wind', and 'the most generous person in the world'—in a rickety canoe on a local creek. The canoe is just a plank supported by kerosene cans. In his *Early Promise* he recalls their voyage. In retrospect, his exultation as they mess about on this ramshackle raft is an intimation of another shore and a greater light.

'Just then I felt a great burst of joy...My happiness ran out in all directions, over the bumpy water, up, up to the grey cloud beyond the bridge, the great knots of it, watery, weepy at the edges, moving slowly across the sky, slowly like we were coming apart a bit, so that through it, there came these gleams of light beyond, so still and sure...streaming out, up there, far beyond the cloud, to shine on the towers, towers of the New Jerusalem, Jerusalem the golden with milk and honey bless'd. You had to work your way towards the light...you had to hold to the promises...The water got heavier as we kept on scooping. So did the clouds. But the patches, the cracks, the streams of light got brighter. Or they would in a moment. It was a promise. We'd reach the other shore' (Burns, 1975, 26).

'It was a promise. We'd reach the other shore.' Our spirituality is 'our awareness of the other and the beyond'. D. R. Burns is not the only writer for whom 'the beyond' is the further bank of a river. We recall little Helen Forrester who cried because she could not cross the Mersey to reach the green fields and wild seashores she loved (Forrester, 1974, 275). And we remember the 'scrap of a song' which Rabindranath Tagore heard as boy, 'Ferryman, take me across to the other shore!' (Tagore, 1913a, 162).

'It was a promise. We'd reach the other shore.' The imagery and the promise of 'another shore and a greater light' is that of the Christian tradition but not of that tradition alone. The testimony of the little Australian boy, the child from a poor Merseyside home, and the child of an aristocratic Bengali family is that the yearning for that other shore is a craving of the spirit that, however little they speak of it, children from every culture know.

I am moved by the resonances between the language of these accounts, describing what on any definition must be recognised as the experience of the spirit of the child, and the understanding of the role of 'the Spirit' in a number of New Testament texts. The experience of the Spirit is of the 'first–fruits' (Romans 8.23), the pledge and the promise of the full harvest. In another image it is the 'first instalment' (2 Corinthians 1.22) of the full payment to come. We must move with caution, but a Christian reading of the experiences we have cited will dare to see them as signs of the Spirit moving where he will.

Epiphany and promise

As for Helen Forrester, as for D. R. Burns, so too for John Raynor, the peak experiences of childhood are promises of what is yet to be. Raynor describes several occasions during his childhood when, as he puts it, 'the veil was for fleeting moments drawn aside'. He recalls an evening of his family holiday in the Cotswolds. He has been out with his net hunting butterflies, when he notices a rare Hummingbird Hawk Moth. He strikes with his net and imagines he must have caught it. But then, to his intense distress, he sees that his net is empty. 'After a time I cried, with the old cry, because I had failed to capture beauty; because it wasn't enough to see it, I wanted it for my own'. This loss proves 'a preparation for what was to come'. He describes how that same evening, he 'saw beauty'.

'I became aware then of the tremendous creative forces that moved through me like a great wind and could tear and shake my being. I

knew that I saw felt and was what few people feel, see, or are; and in a strong, quiet, uplifted ecstasy I gave myself unreservedly to the forces that have moulded, and always will mould, my life.'
He makes his way home.

'I was limp, drained of vitality, filled with a happiness such as I had never known; I had given myself with wholehearted dedication to this beautiful world in which we have our being; that reveals in such moments so clearly that it is but a foretaste of the landscape beyond the high, forbidding gates of our mortality' (Raynor, 1973, 191-193).

The best now is but 'a foretaste' of the best to come. Again we register the echoes of the language of the Christian New Testament. We recall too the memories of Forrest Reid, A.L. Rowse, and Kathleen Raine, who knew themselves to be exiles from a better world. And we think of another who felt at such moments of heightened awareness a longing for 'something more', for a beauty lovelier still. In his great wartime sermon *The Weight of Glory*, C. S. Lewis, spoke of this sense of being 'on the outside of the world, the wrong side of the door' (Lewis, 1949, p 31). Lewis himself, no more than eight years old, knew this longing (Lewis, 1959, 19). We are bound to wonder whether this discontent, this unspoken hankering for they know not what, is not more widely felt among children than might appear.

John Masefield, sure even as a child of a greater life than this, speaks for all children who catch a glimpse of what George MacDonald called 'the high countries'.

'On one wonderful day, when I was little more than five years old, as I stood looking north, over a clump of honeysuckle in flower, I entered that greater life; and that life entered into me with a delight that I can never forget. I found suddenly that I could imagine imaginary beings complete in every detail, with every faculty and possession, and that these imaginations did what I wished for my delight, with an incredible perfection in a brightness not of this world' (Masefield, 1952, 11).

Touched by the transcendent

For some these moments of exaltation—at least as they are recalled—amount to theophanies, disclosures of the divine. Elizabeth Hamilton tells of how, for a brief space, God was with her in the garden.

'Once as I was looking at a calceolaria, fingering the yellow blossom, marvelling at the mouth that opened and shut and the bulbous under-lip speckled with crimson, God was with me in the garden. It was a moment in time and yet out of it. I wanted to prolong it. But I could not. It had passed and I was alone' (Hamilton, 1963, 26-29).

Anne Treneer and her brother play truant from school one day. Through the Cornish sea mist they see a wonderful sight.

'I suppose the sun was trying to come out and the rays were in some way refracted by the mist. We saw a golden light, not brilliant but mellow and suffused, yet with a core of concentrated spendour—a sheaf of gilding. It was the dull but glowing gold of gilded missals... On Dodman Point that day of my childhood, I thought the splendour was God' (Treneer, 1944, 39-40).

We stay in Cornwall and return to one of A. L. Rowse's early memories. He recalls,

'The peculiar purity of the blue sky seen through the white clusters of the apple-blossom in spring. I remember being moon-struck looking at it one morning early on my way to school. It meant something for me; what I couldn't say. It gave me unease at heart, such reaching out towards perfection such as impels men into religion, some sense of the transcendence of things, of the fragility of our hold upon life.'

Rowse describes this experience as 'an early taste of aesthetic sensation, a kind of revelation, which has since become a secret touchstone of experience for me, an inner resource and consolation'. He recognises such experiences as those which Wordsworth records in his *Tintern Abbey* and his *Ode on the Intimations of Immortality*. So important are these experiences to Rowse that the truth-claims of religion are immaterial, for nothing in religion, as he has experienced it, answers to them. As we saw earlier, W. H. Hudson felt the same. Rowse describes movingly his first such intimation, when one still evening he heard the sound of the bells of St. Mewan church across the fields. Rowse's recollection of those bells—'their memory speaks to me of my buried childhood' is marked by a nostalgia which, as we have seen, suffuses page after page of his memoir (Rowse, 1942, 16-18, 85-86). It is, as we cannot overemphasise, the nostalgia *of* childhood, not alone a nostalgia *for* childhood, that touches such pages in our memoirs.

Percy Lubbock, author of *Earlham*—for the present writer, the loveliest of our memoirs of childhood—turns to George Meredith to express both the evanescence and the eternal consequence of these moments out of time.

> "'Of thee to say Behold, has said Adieu": it is true of the rose-glimmer of dawn, it is truer still, I am sorry to find, of these beautiful visitations. Somebody has come into the room, common life shut down upon the child again—so it happened; but so it always happens, I have never discovered the secret of prolonging the few rare moments. Enough that in passing they bestow their imperishable gift; the time, the place, are marked for ever afterwards, plainly to be seen over lengthening years' (Lubbock, 1922, 85).

Disclosure and discipleship

What bearing, if any, do 'peak experiences', such as our writers recall, have on Christian discipleship and the spiritual nurture of children? Spiritual directors of every tradition advise us neither to expect nor to seek ecstatic experiences, even though many of the saints seem to have enjoyed them. We do not become like children by practising mental exercises, by using meditative techniques—or exotic substances—hoping that they will heighten out spiritual awareness so that more of those 'unattended moments' come our way. Christian discipleship is to do with what is required of me, not with how I feel. The more I am away with the angels, it might be said, the further I am from my neighbour. Moreover such experiences cannot be grasped, only received. All we can do, as William Blake recognised, is to 'kiss the joy as it flies'.

We cannot engineer 'peak experiences' for ourselves. Nor can we make them happen for our children. It would be manipulative, even abusive, to try. And yet and yet. If indeed such experiences are not sufficiently explained as unusual mental events—though that at least they are—but are moments of disclosure, then they are to be acknowledged and affirmed as such. We can at least refuse to collude with a culture that discourages mention of them. If there is sufficient openness and trust, a child may sometimes share such moments with us.

We can at least be rather more aware of what is sometimes disclosed to children than Leslie Paul's scoutmaster was. Paul, describes his 'lyric astonishment' when he first met a swallow. For Paul and the other boys of the scout troop he belonged to, the word 'swallow', as his patrol was called, was like the word 'pelican' ('whose beak holds more than his belly can'). The word was a joke. It never occurred to him that such a bird existed. Then one day, out with his scout troop, he sees,

'A regal bird with scything wings and forked tail, rufous breast and purple back was sweeping the downs almost about my feet. The April sun glittered on it as on a swimmer turning in water. It was proud and swift and terrible in its beauty as the Holy Ghost descending like a dove at the Jordan' (Paul, 1946, 11-12).

Gradually he becomes aware of his scoutmaster wittering away nearby. The good man is pedantically insisting that this august being is a swallow. The boy can scarcely be brought to believe that the vision vouchsafed to him can be of a creature so absurdly named.

A teacher at Rabindranath Tagore's school is more sensitive. He remembers an incident in a class he was teaching.

'In the middle of one class I was suddenly interrupted in my teaching by one of the boys calling my attention to the song of a bird in the branches overhead. We stopped the teaching and listened till the bird had finished. It was springtime and the boy who had called my attention to the song said to me, "I don't know why, but somehow

I can't explain what I feel when I hear that bird singing'" (Pearson
and Dey, 1916, 58).

'We stopped the teaching and listened'. Surely that at least we can do.
We can stop and, with them, listen. Perhaps then, occasionally, we too will
catch an echo of what is being said to them.

Certainly how we construe such moments will depend on our prior
understanding of how things are. The Christian understanding of them
will take account of words which serve as commentary on many of the
memories shared with us in this chapter—words which will continue to
sound like a bell throughout this study.

'I thank thee, O Father, Lord of heaven and earth, because thou
hast hid these things from the wise and prudent, and hast revealed
them unto babes. Even so, Father: for so it seemed good in thy sight'
(Matthew 11.25-26).

CHAPTER 7

'BORING JEHOVAH WOULD NOT BUDGE'

In Sunday school a sickly adult
Taught the teachings of a sickly lamb
To a gathering of sickly children.
I cannot recall one elevated moment in church,
Though as a choirboy I pulled in a useful
Sixpence per month.
(Enright, 1973)

God and Jesus

The relationship of religion and spirituality is much debated. This much is uncontested—they are not the same. The disagreement arises over the question of which comes first. For some, religion, understood as the confessional articulation of truth-claims, is primary. Spirituality, on this view, is a dimension of the religious. Spirituality is how a religion expresses itself in the forms of prayer and worship specific to its heritage. On this view, spirituality without a religious anchorage and framework is hopelessly vacuous. For others—probably for most with a mind on these matters—spirituality takes precedence. We are spiritual beings first, innately aware of 'the other and the beyond'. We are religious—if we ever are—only secondly and subsequently. Religion, on this view, voices the spiritual. Traditional religions give us the language and the liturgy with which our spirituality can be expressed. So too do the myriad modern movements—whether newly minted or, so they claim, tapping 'ancient wisdom'—which offer to help us flourish without making us go to church or to any other place of worship.

The premise of this study is that human beings are spiritual, whether or not they are religious. Children are born spiritual. They may or may not experience religion, although until recently most children did. The evidence of our memoirs is that religion can either foster a child's spirituality or stifle it. We wonder why this should be. Why is it that one child's experience of organised religion is enriching while another's is impoverishing? In this chapter we shall try to learn from the bad experiences of religion—and religious people—that some of our memoirists recall. We shall register some of the religious road-blocks that they met on their spiritual journey—aware, as we do so, of Jesus's warning to those who place such obstacles in a child's path. In our next chapter I shall turn to happier memories, to the recollections of writers whose spiritual lives were nourished by the religion of their childhood.

In neatly dividing our testimonies in this way I am of course oversimplifying the evidence. Some of our writers have mixed memories. For some religion simply proves unfit for purpose, failing to articulate either the heights or depths of their spiritual experience. But the broad distinction remains—some adults recall their religious upbringing with gratitude and others with pain, if not with resentment and anger.

I start with the distressing recollections of writers who, as children, sensed the conflict between spirit and letter, between what was real to them and what did not ring true—even though it is only much later that they can they could begin to explain where that contradiction lay.

Geoffrey Dennis, child of a prosperous and respectable Methodist family, accompanies his mother to the church hall where, with the other ladies, she is laying the tables for a special Sunday School tea. Geoffrey wanders into the church by himself and sits in a pew. There this little boy, despite the clatter of plates and tea-cups next-door, is vouchsafed a vision.

'After how long I know not, first a slow mood of mystery, then quicker, of expectation, soon strange extreme expectation, then swift, sweeping over me, overwhelming, a flood of Understanding. Of All: EVERYTHING. Tidal revelation. I know the meaning. I *see*.'

The little boy trots back into the church. ('Forgotten the mystery, forgetting the sacred place'). He trips over and bumps his head. A lady puts butter on the bump that appears. He asks how long he was out of the room. 'Ten minutes,' they say. The adult Dennis comments, 'Untrue: I had been in the empty church forever". And he adds, 'Fifty years passed before I spoke of it to anybody; then only of the lump and butter part, not the secret part'.

It is an arresting instance—told in this writer's impressionistic staccato style—of one of those overwhelming moments of disclosure which we discussed in our last chapter, experiences which count for much but which are rarely shared. It is not the only such moment of exaltation Geoffrey Dennis recalls. Such experiences testify powerfully to the perception of transcendence granted to many children. It is an acuity which, alas, too often fades with the passing of the years.

But young Geoffrey has a problem, a dilemma which only as an adult will he be able to articulate. How is he to relate such vivid experiences of God, as he is sure they are, with what he has been taught about God?

'For with Him these experiences had somehow to do. How precisely, I could not make out; how the presence of God vouchsafed in these sessions joined up with Jehovah, the Almighty of religion and Bible fame. I tried to merge them, to join this ghostly feeling of Him, holy and inly, to the Sinai shape; to combine, coalesce the two.

I could not. Grey Jehovah always took the centre of the stage, demanded all attention...I just had to stare at that God, the cloudy bearded one, and meantime lost the Other. Not only could I not solve the *mysterium* and unite them, I could never get the two present together. Boring Jehovah would not budge; God-Ghostliness faded before Him.'

The child's experience as the adult describes it is striking. With his mother busy with the tea-tables next door, the child meets 'the Other'. The mode of the meeting is 'holy and inly'. Such, we recall, was another child's encounter with the divine. Samuel too had much the same difficulty in persuading the professionally religious to take him seriously (1 Samuel 3).

Dennis's experiences, ('these Hide-and-Seek games of the Eternal') are of the Other. The Other's presence is evanescent and, with a sad inevitability, it yields to the God of religion, 'the Moses bulk and beard', as Dennis calls him. Then, despite the boy's best efforts to bring him back, even that God goes too.

The child Dennis's relationship, such as it is, with religion's 'boring Jehovah' has little to do with Jesus. Although he realises that Jesus is God's son and so must be 'mixed up with Church, religion, holiness', 'in practice He belonged to a different world, tenderer brighter; less mysterious, less dreadful'. 'God lurked dimly, hard to see or fix; Jesus appeared sunlight clear the instant you thought of him' (Dennis, 1957, 130-135).

Unlike God, Jesus appeared 'sunlight clear'. More than once in our memoirs we meet this preference for Jesus, who is accessible and attractive, over the figure called 'God', who is both impenetrable and intimidating. William Woodruff, who grew up in a desperately poor Lancashire mill-town family, attended a Roman Catholic school where the contrast between God and Jesus was embodied in the conflicting personalities and pedagogic styles of those who taught him.

Two nuns shared his religious education, Sister Lucy and Sister Loyola. 'Everyone loved the twinkling, big-boned, innocent Sister Lucy whose face was like a polished apple. I took an instant dislike to the gnarled, thin-lipped Sister Loyola'. Then there was the big-bellied Father Prendergast, 'a kind man who didn't seem to have any purpose other than to tell tales in a slow mellow voice and make fun'. There was no laughter when Sister Loyola visited their class. 'She was as serious as Father Prendergast was jolly. She had suffering on the brain.'

The impressions the child receives from Sister Lucy and Father Prendergast on the one hand and from Sister Loyola on the other imprint a lasting conflict in his mind between God and Jesus. The wedge driven in childhood creates enduring confusion. The adult Woodruff recalls Sister Loyola:

> 'She left me with a life-long fear of God. I didn't fear Christ. He had given his life for others, and as far as I could tell, was a good man who was now quite dead. He was the Good Shepherd. He was real; I knew Him. God was different. He was a strange figure who could pop up anywhere at any time. I never understood why God had sacrificed His son instead of Himself' (Woodruff, 2011, 144-147).

Elisaveta Fen tells us that, as a child, she distinguished Jehovah, 'the God of the Jews', as she called him, from Jesus, 'the God of the Christians'.

The former 'did frightful things to his people'. Jesus, by contrast, was 'gentle and forgiving'. 'Even if His Father was still somewhere in the background, watching us, ready to punish, His Son was also there, to plead on our behalf' (Fen, 1961, 167).

Elisaveta suffered from bad dreams as a child ('Terror pierced me from head to foot') and she prays to be delivered from them. She is inclined to plead with Jesus rather than God.

'I began to wonder whether God was really kind. The Ten Commandments, anyway, sounded as if they came from someone very stern, and the old man with a long white beard, his feet resting on clouds, whom I saw on icons in church, looked rather forbidding. Jesus Christ, I knew, was kind: there was a picture of Him in one of my books, surrounded by children, and saying to the grown-ups in the background: "Let the children come unto Me..." But perhaps, being God's Son, He could not help me without His Father's permission' (Fen, 1961, 139).

Don Haworth, who grew up among the moors and mills of Lancashire in the 1920s and 30s remembers his childhood as fraught with danger. 'The best safeguard'—this he learned early on—'was to cultivate the friendship of Jesus'. At Sunday School a collection was taken. Young Don supposed it was for Jesus.

'God lived in the chapel next door and we did not want him to collar the money. He was frightening. He could see you under the table. He knew everything you did or thought. For two pins he would come down on you like a ton of bricks. Jesus was a different cup of tea. He had a kindly face, performed tricks and had been extensively photographed with lambs, donkeys and multi-racial infants. For a consideration he would fend God off and not have you sunk at sea' (Haworth, 1986, 14).

Images of Jesus and God conflict. Equally confusing for some children is the contradiction between what adults would have them believe and their own moral and spiritual intuitions. Emma Smith makes friends with a boy she meets on the beach, an orphan from the Newquay Barnardo's home. Her mother, when she finds out, is enraged. Emma is bewildered.

'I hadn't been getting up to any mischief, or up to anything else. I'd made a friend; that was all. My vision blurs and my ears buzz with the despair of not understanding what it is that I have done wrong. Yes—I did invite him, Terry, into our beach hut, and yes, I was inside the hut with him when he took off his jersey and shorts and put on Jim's bathing costume...Why was it so very bad?' (Smith, 2008, 106)

Helen Flexner, daughter of an American Quaker family, remembers her bewilderment and distress when her father allows her younger brother Frank to have a sip of wine, although he has 'taken the pledge'. She is appalled by her parents' apparent moral compromise (Flexner, 1940, 67-69).

Eleanor Acland (the 'Milly' of her memoir) was unable to reconcile what she was taught with what she knew in her heart. Religion pinioned her soaring spirit. The religion of her privileged household was a narrow orthodoxy and, in the hands of her grim nurse Barley, it was a rod with which to beat her. Eleanor Acland looks back on the faith of her home as essentially that of the Manichees. All is ordered into two realms, the pleasant and mentionable over against the unpleasant and unmentionable. As a child, she is unable to understand 'on what principle the boundary between the two realms is drawn' (Acland, 1935, 144). She feared 'that she herself was one of the everlasting damned' (122). Her sense of sin and its fatal consequences, of the reality of hell and the inevitability of judgement, is compounded by what she is made to feel is her own delinquency.

But she also develops a growing awareness of the discrepancies and inconsistencies in the orthodox account of things, not to speak of all that is morally repugnant in that system, such as what she is given to understand is the fate of unbaptised babies. Acland's autobiography *Good-bye for the Present* directly addresses the conflict, experienced by Geoffrey Dennis and by many of our writers as children, between the claims and demands of formal religion and the child's own finely tuned spiritual awareness of 'the other', what Acland memorably describes as her 'in-seeing'. Acland relates how as a child she resolved this conflict by 'putting God to the test'.

'Milly took a deep breath, clenched her hands, and there, under the grand open arch of the sky, said loudly and slowly: "Listen to me. I don't care. I'm going to hell. You can't do worse to me. So now I tell You. I just simply hate You. You are crueller than Barley lets Sarah be to a spider." Now let the thunderbolt fall from heaven on the furious child'. (Sarah is Milly's sister.)

But no thunderbolt fell. Then Milly becomes aware of 'a faint but unmistakeable fragrance'. '"White violets!" she exclaimed. They are the 'dearest of spring flowers'. The adult Eleanor Acland adds,

'The child had dashed her puny fist in the face of the invisible Love; and Love, undisturbed and unoffended, continued to smile upon her and to guide her feet out of the shadow of death into the way of peace' (184-187).

Love still smiled on the child—a love which cannot be defeated by the awful things religion can do.

Our memoirs suggest that institutional religion blocks the child's spiritual path in at least three ways, though any such analysis is bound to be clumsy. Here we must speak plainly of what we adults—you and I—have done to children. First, we have bored them. Secondly, we have not made sense to them. Thirdly, we have put them off by the kind of people we are. We have been the inhuman face of God.

The endless dreary sermon

'Milly'—Mary Acland—found church boring. It was, she tells us, 'an affair of the grown-ups' and its services 'in no way made a path for us towards a God whom we could understand, worship, or love'. Only the sound of the organ means anything to her (Acland, 1935, 159-160).

John Raynor was unusually open to 'the other and the beyond', but the liturgy of Westminster Abbey, exemplary as no doubt it was, did little to nourish his ardent spirituality. His mother took him to the morning service at the Abbey. 'It was a long service,' he tells us, 'two hours—and

I disliked it intensely...The droning voices of the canons as they read the lessons, the interminable prayers, and above all the endless dreary sermon...all weighed heavily on my youthful restlessness'. He adds—he and Mary Acland are kindred spirits—'Only the singing I liked' (Raynor, 1973, 11).

William Magan was a child of the 'Ascendancy', the network of Protestant English families who had been the lords of Irish lands since the end of the seventeenth century. He went on to be a Brigadier and a Master of Foxhounds. As a child he found Sunday, 'the most boring day of the week'. Sunday clothes were tight and uncomfortable and games permitted on weekdays were forbidden. The child's religious life was ruled by his mother whose God was 'tyrannical old Jehovah', a god who, the child notes, does not laugh. He enjoyed walking to church, because their route involved scaling wooden steps over a high wall, which was 'a mild adventure and fun'. In church, the hymns were 'all right', but the rest he found 'unutterably tedious' (Magan, 1996, 95-98).

Mary Acland, John Raynor, Wiliam Magan—all three find much of divine worship suffocatingly dreary. But for all three the tedium is relieved by music. As we have seen, the spiritual cannot be separated from the sensory. In church these children suffer nothing short of sensory deprivation—until, that is, *sound*, the sound of the organ or the sound of singing lifts their spirit. We shall see in Chapter Nine how significant music can be in a child's spiritual formation.

Theatrical and incomprehensible

Many writers tell us that they found the claims of religion unintelligible. The young Russian boy Konstantin Paustovsky attends a night-time Mass, celebrated by a cardinal in a monastery, where a miraculous icon of the virgin is preserved. He tells us this was his 'first encounter with religious fanaticism'. 'I had never before seen anything so theatrical and incomprehensible,' he recalls. He refuses to do as his grandmother tells him and kiss the cardinal's cassock. Instead, 'pale with resentment', he stares straight in the cardinal's face (Paustovsky, 1964, 32-36).

Frank McCourt's memories remind us that much of religion is simply indecipherable to the child. His father takes him to church 'where all the priests wear white and sing'.

'They are happy because our Lord is in heaven. I ask Dad if the baby in the crib is dead and he says, No, He was thirty-three when he died and there he is hanging on the cross. I don't understand how he grew up so fast that He's hanging there with a hat made of thorns and blood everywhere, dripping from His head, His hands, His feet, and a big hole near His belly' (McCourt, 1997, 118).

At school he is subjected to prurient sermons from a Redemptorist priest about the sixth commandment and 'impurity'. ('Resist the devil and keep your hands to yourself.') In confession, he admits, 'I did dirty things.' The priest enquires whether that was 'with yourself, or with another, or with some class of beast?' McCourt adds, '"Some class of beast." I never heard of a sin like that before. This priest must be from the country and, if he is, he's opening up new worlds to me' (340-342).

In fairness we must add that not all the priests McCourt encounters are gross or comic. Desperately hungry, he steals some fish and chips. When he confesses his sin, the priest is silent.

'I wonder if this priest is asleep because he's very quiet till he says, "My child, I sit here. I hear the sins of the poor. I assign penance. I bestow absolution. I should be on my knees washing their feet"' (208-209).

The furtive she-evangelist Miss Crouch

What a child makes of religion and how helpful it is in their spiritual development depend crucially on religion's representatives, on parents, clergy, and teachers and others who are—as I shall call them—'the faces of faith' to them. Children reject the religion taught them by those they have every reason to despise. Equally, as we shall see in our next chapter, a child's response to religion will be encouraged by those they love. Then religion smiles on the child and serves the child's flourishing.

In few of our memoirs is the religious sundered quite so sharply from the spiritual as in Forrest Reid's *Apostate*. In his imagination Reid inhabits another world altogether more real to him than that of his monotonous Belfast boyhood. He rages against religion. 'I hated Sunday, I hated Sunday School, I hated Bible stories, I hated everybody mentioned in both the Old and New Testaments, except perhaps the impenitent thief, Eve's snake, and a few similar characters' (Reid, 1947, 19). He is repelled by the attentions of Mr Farrington, the curate ('low church, evangelical, uncouth') and of 'the furtive she-evangelist Miss Crouch' (100-105).

Alas, Mr Farrington and Miss Crouch are not the only such forbidding figures we meet. Frances Donaldson grew up in south London in the 1920s. Her experience of the professionally religious left her permanently embittered. Although, as we have seen, she claimed to be an unimaginative child, she was well able to recognise that the clergyman ministering to her Sunday by Sunday was a disgrace to his cloth. She went to church ('of a Low Church kind') in suburban London. The vicar, she tells us,

'was a very tall, shabby, old man, and almost gaga...He sniffed constantly and a permanent small stream of saliva flowed down to his chin. Every Sunday morning he indulged himself for half an hour in the pulpit. This was the most agonising experience of the whole of my school days...I developed a burning hatred for this old man, which I think accounts for the fact that I can never enter a church during a service without my hackles beginning to rise' (Donaldson, 1959, 54).

Some children eventually see through a religious upbringing which demanded no more of them than that they comply with a code, the particular schedule of requirements that their church or sect imposed. Patricia Beer (like Paul Ashton) recalls growing up in a Plymouth Brethren family and how the beliefs and attitudes of the Brethren, which she uncritically accepted, shaped every aspect of her life. She gives us a memorably mordant account of how their services seemed to her as a child, services which, she concedes, she on the whole enjoyed. Eventually she came to realise that her faith was largely a consequence of conditioning. Her judgement on the Plymouth Brethren's 'entirely negative code of behaviour' is damning. 'I really cannot think of any virtue, as opposed to outward behaviour, which the Brethren extolled or tried to inculcate in their children and practised themselves' (Beer, 1978, 119).

Among our memoirs it is sad to come across examples of the baleful influence of some Christian missionaries on the spiritual life of children. Two examples must suffice.

The Japanese writer Yoshio Markino's experience was particularly unfortunate and we must hope that it was untypical. Yoshio went to a mission school so that he could learn English. There he is pressured into being baptized. He reads the Bible for himself and is soon asking questions. For example, he wonders what is the fate of those who died before the coming of Christ. The missionaries fob him off, blaming him for having read too many 'bad books'. He is appalled by the missionaries' parsimony, by their hypocrisy, and by their sectarianism. And by worse. The 'head missionary' imports a young wife.

'During the lesson hours in the classroom the wife was always sitting on her husband's lap, and they embraced each other and were kissing all the time, so busy to kiss that the teacher could not answer to the questions by the students' (Markino, 1912, 111-112).

Paulias Matane grew up in a remote village in Papua New Guinea in the 1930s. The life of the village life was permeated by the spiritual, by the presence and intervention of the spirits, benevolent or malign, and by the 'Tubuan' magic powers by which the good spirits were summoned and the evil spirits driven away. Then one day a Christian pastor appears and builds a church to which he summons the boys for lessons. He denounces Tubuan ways. He speaks 'in the name of our Father in the clouds'. He insists that they take a bath in the river before they come to school and he makes them march up and down like soldiers. All of which the boys find totally confusing. (Matane, 1972, 64-67).

Thank God, the wells of the spirit are not easily capped. Our memoirs testify to resilience of the child's spirit and the power of that spirit to prevail over their bad experiences of religious practices and—often just as lethal—religious people.

The questioning child

Religion militates against spirituality when it fails to take seriously the questions a spirited child asks. The questioning child finds that he or she is having to choose between the 'answers', such as they are, that religion offers and the promptings of the spirit within.

Elisaveta Fen is bewildered that God does not answer her prayer to be delivered from her terrible dreams. 'Could God be punishing me for something I had done?' she asks herself. She begins to wonder whether God is really kind. Her mother tells her to recite 'the Resurrection prayer'. The prayer works for a while but not for long. She wonders whether the reason her prayer for the dreams to stop is not being answered is because she does not have enough faith. Faith can move mountains, she reads. She tries, on this basis, to make the door move. It doesn't. So she begins to doubt the truth of what she has been taught.

'The discovery that my faith was inadequate, although I felt it to be fervent and strong, became itself a seed of doubt. The doubt was too vague to be put into words, but its effects were insidious: I was no longer sure that the things I was told even by my mother, or read, even in the book of Holy Stories in the Gospels, really meant what they said. I made the discovery of scepticism' (Fen, 1961, 174-179).

Some children begin thinking about what it all means while they are still small. We saw earlier how Jill Ker Conway, child of the Australian outback, is distressed and bewildered by nature's cruelty, by the fact that the world seems organised so that the strong prey on the weak. Receiving no answers to the questions that torment her, she begins to question the traditional religious account of things. As a devastating drought takes its toll, her brother quotes from Shakespeare's *King Lear*, 'As flies to wanton boys are we to the Gods/ They kill us for our sport'. Conway adds,

'I did not understand the nature of the ecological disaster which had transformed my world, or that we ourselves had been agents as well as participants in our own catastrophe. I just knew that we had been defeated by the fury of the elements, a fury that I could not see we had earned' (Conway, 1998, 82).

So she refuses to be confirmed.

'To my own experience of disaster at Coorain, I now added the pictures of Belsen and Dachau, and the chilling photographs of Hiroshima and Nagasaki. While these might well have convinced me of the truth of original sin, they served me at the time as further confirmation of the malign nature of the fates, and reinforced my sense of religious faith as a sentimental illusion' (114).

Ernest Hillen was brought up on a tea plantation in Java. When the Japanese invade the Dutch East Indies in 1942 all European families are interned and the child's idyllic life is brought to an abrupt end. He is obliged to witness unspeakable brutality. As best they can, the internees celebrate Christmas with a make-do party. They gather round to hear the formidable Mrs Witte read the Christmas story, a narrative that prompts this sensitive child to ask some searching questions.

'Jesus, when he was older, said we should love everybody...But what about the Japanese? They were the enemy! My mother had said so, again and again. But Jesus had especially mentioned enemies. Had He ever been in a camp though? Had he seen the Japanese beating women and girls? (Hillen, 1995, 62-63)

One thoughtful nineteenth-century child conducted a bold experiment to ascertain whether what he had been told about God was true. Edmund Gosse's parents were members of the Plymouth Brethren. (His father was Philip Gosse, a marine zoologist of great repute, whose belief that the world was created in seven days some few thousand years previously was not threatened by his meticulous scientific observations.) In his celebrated memoir *Father and Son*, Edmund Gosse describes how one morning he bowed down to worship a chair that he had hoisted on to a table. He fully expected God to respond in some way to this act of idol-atry. But nothing happened. The effect of this experiment is not at this point to undermine the child's belief in God. The doubts will come later. But the boy does conclude that his father 'was not really acquainted with the Divine practice in cases of idolatry' (Gosse, 1983, 66-67).

Some of our writers recognise that, while they were still children, the religious was already in potential conflict with the spiritual in its failure to do justice to their experience of the transcendent.

At the age of eight the novelist Antonia White was sent away to board at the Convent of the Sacred Heart, Roehampton. In her classic account of her schooldays *Frost in May* (White, 1933), the Convent of the Sacred Heart is renamed as 'The Convent of the Five Wounds'. *Frost in May* is a novel but it speaks directly from the author's own experience. The protagonist of the novel Nanda is Antonia herself. Nanda accepts without question—indeed she embraces with enthusiasm—the fevered Catholic piety that permeates the school, seeking to outdo her peers in the intensity of her devotions. But Nanda comes to delight too in music and poetry. Another pupil gives her a volume of Francis Thompson's poetry as a First Communion present and she is enraptured by what she reads. She is enchanted by Augustine's words and repeats them to herself over and over again, 'Too late have I loved thee, O Beauty ancient and ever new'.

Nanda's dutiful observance of what her religion requires is initially unaffected by her dawning love for all things beautiful. But a tension is created that will eventually end in conflict.

'But only very rarely and by extreme concentration could she ever obtain from any religious exercise the pure delight that poetry or music aroused without the least effort on her part. Quite sincerely she tried to make religion the centre of her life, but to do so required constant watchfulness and direction of her will. She tried to persuade herself that her love of beauty was connected with God...but some small, clear, irritating voice assured her that it was an independent growth'(157).

The child's faith will survive for a little longer, but finally it will falter and then founder because it does not resonate with the poetry and music which moves her much more deeply.

Antonia White's *Frost in May* belongs to a genre of memoir that arguably deserves a study of its own, the memoir of childhood in a convent school. I draw attention to just two further such autobiographies.

Juliet M. Soskice was the youngest sibling of the writer Ford Madox Ford, the granddaughter of the artist Ford Madox Brown, and the niece of the painter Dante Gabriel Rossetti and the poet Christina Rossetti. Unsurprisingly, her childhood was unconventional. She was brought up by another aunt and uncle who were anarchists and by the age of eight little Juliet considered herself an anarchist too. Yet she is sent to a convent school. Her graphic account of life in this school and of the terrifying doctrines drilled into her there—limbo, purgatory, and hell are 'hot, hotter, and hottest'—is made all the more compelling by the cool tone in which it is told. Soskice's story is the oft-told tale of loss of faith, but nowhere in our literature is that loss more sudden and dramatic. Doubts have long been crowding in, but her faith finally collapses like a house of cards at the very moment of her first communion. She has difficulty in swallowing the host—then,

'As it went down it left a flavour in my mouth like that of the wafers that are eaten with ices, and when I tasted that I suddenly felt sure it was not Christ' (Soskice, 1994, 129).

Soskice's memorable testimony invites a more extended commentary than the limits of this essay allow. But four factors can be identified to suggest why for this child religion should have so failed the spirit. First, the literalism of traditional Roman Catholic claims, as they were presented to her, bewilders and terrifies her. She once burned her hand on the kitchen stove at home. Can hell be as painful? Secondly, she cannot forget her irreligious grandfather whom she loves deeply. Surely, she asks, he too cannot be doomed to eternal flames? Thirdly, there was Father G.—one of a gallery of appalling or alarming priests and religious whom we meet in this memoir—who 'waddled about with his small eyes turned up to heaven and his fat cheeks shaking like jellies. He was protrudant in front and gabbled off the mass as quickly as though he had not a moment to waste and was anxious to get home to breakfast' (110). Such 'faces of faith', as I have called them, repel the child's spirit. But the spectacle that tips the scales for Janet at her first communion is that of the sacristan dusting the tabernacle with a feather brush as though it were a piece of furniture. (To be sure, not all the priests Janet meets are as unappealing as Father G. There was Father W. who 'never told us about the horrors of hell, but always about the joy of heaven' (91).) Fourthly, and most fundamentally, the religion she has been taught fails this child's spirit, not only because it avoids questions, but—much more seriously—because it explicitly warns against even asking them. She is taught that to persist in asking questions is to commit the sin of audacity and that even to secretly wonder, even to ask yourself a question, is a want of reverence.

Janet Soskice cannot accept that her kind but unbelieving grandfather, whom she loves so much, is condemned to hell. Nor can little Mary McCarthy—who will one day become one of America's most distinguished novelists—accept that her upright Presbyterian grandfather is similarly bound for hell, his inescapable doom if the enthusiastic Jesuit preaching at her catholic boarding school is to be believed.

> 'How could it be that my grandfather, the most virtuous person I knew, whose name was a byword among his friends and colleagues for a kind of rigid and fantastic probity—how could it be that this man should be lost, while I, the object of his admonition, the despair of his example—I, who yielded to every impulse, led, boasted, betrayed—should, by virtue of regular attendance at the sacraments and the habit of easy penitence, be saved?' (McCarthy 1963, 78-79)

For the young W. H. Hudson the inadequacy of religion as he experienced it was its failure to move him as nature did. As a boy Hudson believed implicitly in what he had been taught about 'the Supreme Being'. 'But apart from the fact that the powers above would save me in the end from extinction, which was a great consolation, these teachings did not touch my heart as it was touched and thrilled by something nearer, more intimate, in nature.'

Such testimonies show how religion fails the child when it fails to acknowledge and endorse all that the child delights in. The obligation of religion to the spiritual—dishonoured in the experience of the writers I have been citing in this chapter—is to affirm that all our joys at any age spring from a single source.

'Woe unto the world because of offences!'

This chapter has been painful to write. We have seen how both the rites of religion and, still more damagingly, the representatives of religion have come close to quenching the child's spirit.

Adults, who lead more or less interesting lives, forget what it is to be bored. Adults, who can usually make sense of what is said to them, forget what it is to be addressed unintelligibly. Adults, whose questions are heard if not always answered, forget what it is to have their questions ignored or dismissed. Adults, who have become inured to hypocrisy and half-truths, forget how bitterly pretence and insincerity once bewildered and injured them. Adults, who are on the whole free to avoid the company of the egregiously unpleasant, forget what it once was to have been at their mercy.

We tremble at words said to us about millstones.

CHAPTER 8

Laughter and Prayers

The setting sun has turned the Irrawaddy to molten gold. I pause on the terrace of a busy little temple on the river bank. Here's where you come as the sun goes down. You come to make your devotions. You come to sit and talk. You come to be. There's no hurry to be anywhere else. The temple is the children's playground. A boy and girl—seven or eight-year-olds, I'd guess—have invented a splendid game. The girl sits and stretches out a leg and the boy jumps over it. Then she balances the heel of one foot on the big toe of the other to make a two-barred gate for him to jump over. Then out comes an arm and she's a three-barred gate for him to clear. Next, with the other arm out, she's a four-barred gate and once more the boy leaps over. Bubbling with laughter, they tumble over each other beneath the benevolent figure of the Buddha. Suddenly they break off their game, trot up to the Buddha, kneel side by side before him, and touch their foreheads to the floor. Then, sitting up and at the top of their voices, they break into a chant. Then it's straight back to their game. Play has passed into prayer and prayer has passed into play. And I think sadly of all that in the West we have lost.

South and East

The religious and the spiritual need not be enemies, as the above extract from my diary shows. In this chapter we share memories of how they can be mutually supportive, of how religion can lend voice to the spirit and how the spirit can breathe life into religion's dry bones.

For most of humanity for most of its history, the religious and the spiritual have been one. Many of our memoirs testify to the symbiosis of what we have separated, notably those which recall growing up in cultures and communities on which secularist assumptions and western ways had not yet impacted. There, beyond our reach, we do not find that the religious and the spiritual are in conflict and there we shall begin.

Camara Laye, born in 1928, remembers growing up in an African village in what is now Ghana. For this little boy all of life was steeped in the spiritual. The world of the spirit was not another realm intermittently encroaching on his own, but a constant dimension of his everyday experience. The child's world is populated by spirits, as much *there* as members of his own family. 'What were these guiding spirits,' he asks, 'that I encountered almost everywhere, forbidding one thing, commanding another to be done?' (Laye, 1959, 16).

Laye describes how his father called upon the spirits to come to his aid in his work as a goldsmith.

> 'Were they not the spirits of fire and gold, of fire and air, air breathed through the earthen pipes, of fire born of air, of gold married with fire—were not these the spirits he was invoking?' (26).

In the east, at least where the west has not poisoned its ancient wells, religion and spirituality remain at one. Mulk Raj Anand, who grew up in India, writes of his early memories of the crowded highway along which his father's regiment moved with all its baggage. (Much the same impression was made on Rudyard Kipling's Kim as he travelled the Grand Trunk Road.) The myths and legends of the gods, told him by his mother, blend with the traffic of the road.

> 'I picked up, from under the pupils of my eyes, vague visions of those fabulous figures like the giants and demons into which the clouds formed and reformed over my head as I was put down to bed in the courtyard of our house. And sometimes I contemplated with an immobile stare, filled with wonder and horror, the immobility of one of those almighty chimeras, with heads like the stumps of carrots or pumpkins. And there were no standards to check my imaginings about the humanity which had passed down this road, except that the outlines of the figures were suggested by the medley of sights and sounds that I had experienced up to the age

of five years. *And yet there was no confusion in my muddled fantasy world'* (Anand, 2005, 51). (My italics)

Religion did not sow seeds of confusion in the mind of this spiritually sensitive child, as, alas, it did in the minds of many of the children we met in our last chapter.

Anand describes the fervent, intense, all-pervading spirituality of his Sikh uncles' household where 'the housetops seemed to be vibrating with laughter and prayers' (189-191). 'Laughter and prayers'—much is said in those three words about a marriage that endures in the East but which, in the West, is imperilled where it is not already dissolved.

'Laughter and prayers' characterised the religion of Tsewang Pemba's Tibetan childhood.

'Religion certainly plays an important part in the lives of Tibetans, but it does not prevent them getting fun out of life. They take their religion seriously but also with a sense of humour. Moreover their religion is wide, tolerant to an astonishing degree, and has no strict finicky rules and regulations. From our youngest days we were surrounded in our homes by a religious atmosphere which is not found in the homes of Western countries. Every Tibetan home, no matter how poor, has a private chapel' (Pemba, 1957, 26).

In the communities recalled in the canonical Russian memoirs of childhood of Serghei Aksakoff and Maxim Gorky, the Orthodox Church is at life's centre, less a backdrop to life than its beating heart. All that is experienced, for good or ill, is interpreted by the light and language of faith. When the harvest fails and the reaper is confronted by a field of thistles and weeds, the response is to say, 'It is God's will.' Aksakoff adds that these simple words 'calm all agitation and check all human murmurings, and under their beneficent power Orthodox Russia lives to this day' (Aksakoff, 1923, 215-16).

In Maxim Gorky's portrait of his unforgettable grandmother, we meet religion at its most attractive. 'She's a kind of a saint, your granny,' says the old servant Grigori, 'even if she does take a drop now and then and likes her snuff. You hold tight to her, sonny' (Gorky, 1961, 55). For the boy's grandmother the practice of her faith—her immersion in the Orthodox liturgy, her devotion to the saints, her hours before the icons—provides a conduit for all her griefs, longings, and joys. But she does find life puzzling, we're told. 'It's a tangled piece of lace-making, Alyosha,' she says, 'done by a blind old woman; no wonder you and me can't make head or tail of it' (60). The child overhears her endless voluble prayers. 'Sometimes it seemed to me,' Gorky comments, 'that she played with the icons as seriously and sincerely as my cousin Katerina with her dolls' (70-76).

'She played with the icons.' Prayer passes into play and play into prayer. We pause to register the resonances of Gorky's comment and to ponder its implications for the nurture of the spirit and for our own discipleship. In playful prayer and prayerful play religion and spirituality are one.

Maxim's grandfather's religion is a chilling contrast to the faith and practice of his grandmother. His grandfather writes 'Thou shalt not' across everything the child enjoys. On Saturday evenings, grandfather goes to church—but only after first thrashing the children who had sinned during the week (44). Maxim's grandfather's God is always angry.

'Whenever grandfather told me about the strong arm of God, he emphasised its ruthlessness: once, for example, when people sinned they were drowned in a flood; another time their cities were burned and destroyed; God punished people by famine and plague; He was always a raised sword, a lash for the wicked' (136).

Gorky tells us that his crucial discovery was recognising that his grandparents worshipped two different Gods. 'At a very early date, I realized that my grandfather had one God, my grandmother another' (127).

'My grandfather took me to church: on Saturday to vespers, on Sundays to late mass. Even at church I could tell which God people prayed to: the priest and the deacon prayed to grandfather's God, but the choir always sang to grandmother's' (140).

The boy remembers that the contrast between the different divinities his grandparents worshipped caused him much spiritual conflict. But ultimately it is his relationship with his grandmother which prevails.

That relationship proves spiritually and morally formative. Both his understanding of God and the habits of his moral life are shaped by what he sees in her.

> 'Yet she did not utter the name of God as often as my grandfather. I could understand my grandmother's God and was not afraid of Him, yet I could not lie in His presence—it would have been shameful. Because of this shame I never lied to my grandmother. It was simply impossible to hide anything from so kind a God, and I do not think I had the slightest intention to do so' (130).

Gorky's description of the two faces of religion he saw in his grandparents is of the first importance for us. For good or ill, it is after our likeness that our children fashion their image of God.

The language of the spirit

We do not have to go to Africa or India, to Russia or Tibet, to find places where the spiritual and religious are integral to each other and to all of life. Most of the memoirs we have turned to in this study are from the English-speaking world. In pockets of rural England centuries-old attitudes and assumptions prevailed until well into twentieth century, even though the writers who grew up in those regions recognised that the world they described was fast disappearing. Most country children said their prayers when they went to bed. Most went to church with their families on Sundays. The familiar religious structures, the drama of worship, the rhythm of the church seasons, and the mother-tongue of a religious language learned from birth—all these enriched their lives. The vocabulary of faith took up and celebrated what, before words and beyond words, most mattered to them. Religion gave voice to their spirit.

Among the most celebrated of twentieth century autobiographies of childhood is Laurie Lee's *Cider with Rosie*. His classic account of growing up in a Gloucestershire village makes little direct reference to the religious or the spiritual, yet clearly there is a dimension to the common life of his community that is both. Lee recalls Sunday services in his village church.

'In the packed congregation solemnity ruled. There was power, lamentation, full-throated singing, heavy prayers, and public repentance. No one in the village stayed away without reason, and no one yet wished to do so. We had come to the church because it was Sunday, just as we washed our clothes on Monday...This morning service was also something else. It was a return to the Ark of all our species in the face of the everlasting flood. We are free of that need now and when the flood does come (we) shall drown proud and alone, no doubt. As it was, the lion knelt down with the lamb, the dove perched on the neck of the hawk, sheep nuzzled wolf, we drew warmth from one another and knew ourselves beasts of one kingdom' (Lee, 1959, 219-220).

Like Laurie Lee, Richard Hillyer grew up in rural poverty. His father was a farm labourer. His life as a child was almost entirely confined to his village and the surrounding countryside. The cycle of the seasons and the demands of the land governed everyone's life. And religion was the hub to that cycle.

'Religion was the pivot on which we turned. There it was, fixed, immovable, both controlling us and encouraging us, giving us an importance we shouldn't have had without it. Religion supplied the literature, philosophy, music and drama of a population, the bulk of which could barely read' (Hillyer, 1966, 33).

'Dim and confused though the notion of religion might be, it held back despair. We might have been dumb animals, mere beasts of burden, so far as our ordinary life was concerned, but in church or chapel we knew that we were not' (42).

Ida Gandy grew up in a Wiltshire vicarage. She falls naturally into religious language to voice her delight in a secluded corner of their garden. She refers to 'the heavenly blue of the larkspurs' and to 'the saintliness of the lilies' (Gandy, 1929, 32). Ida and the other children love their beautiful old church. For them it is 'a perpetual symbol, to minds troubled by disordered dreams, of peace and safety' (63). She recalls what the church bells meant for her. 'Their music, reaching us when we stood on some far summit of the downs, would waken such strange longings in us as could never be put into words' (70).

Her exultation in the wonder of their world sometimes passes into prayer.

> 'Sometimes, particularly at sunset time, when the spire appeared to be made of gold, and there was gold on the breasts of the swallows above us, and such a splendour of red and gold in the west that it seemed like music—why, then, though it was not the proper time for prayers, you could not help praying—praying unconsciously with eyes wide open' (72).

'With eyes wide open'. We note those words. Ida's prayer does not comply with the pattern of prayer adults have traditionally imposed on children—'Hands together, eyes closed'. Children do not pray better when their senses are shut down. Sight with two eyes becomes spiritual perception and—eyes still open—passes into prayer. Ida's prayer is not verbalised. We are told that, for those far advanced on the spiritual path, prayer passes beyond words. If so, perhaps one day we shall once again pray as we did as children.

Ida Gandy lives in tune with the church seasons—though on Good Friday there is a discord to be resolved. In the morning she listens and takes to heart 'the almost too familiar tale of the sufferings of Christ' (153). But in the afternoon, by immemorial tradition, she and her siblings search the downs for flowers with which to decorate the church for Easter. She describes how, once high on the downs, their spirits rose. They were back in their own world again.

> 'That other world, where sad-looking people stood under a cross and let Christ's blood "drop gently on them drop by drop", ceased to exist for us... *This* was the real world'.

Gandy describes how they 'turned somersaults in the grass or leaped the juniper bushes', how they 'buried their noses in great clusters of gorse blossom', and how finally, having filled their baskets with flowers, their thoughts turned to tea.

At last they must turn for home, and, as they do so, they hear the church bells and they recall that it is still Good Friday. They heed this summons without resentment. Ultimately there is no contradiction between the religious and the spiritual, between the day's oft-told story and the exaltation and enchantment they have experienced.

'We knew as we trudged along through the dust that (the bells) were calling us too, but we heard them without dismay; we even found something pleasant in the subdued melancholy with which they filled the air. We had had our day; we had been one with the joyful riot of spring…These delights were over now and we were tired and incapable of further deep emotion. The church was our friendly angel again, welcoming us home. We would rest quietly under her dim arches, and join in the long slow hymns, warmed by their gentle sentiment to offer, without rebellion, without even conscious humbug, our souls and bodies to the service of Christ' (162).

To read such a passage today is well-nigh heartbreaking, knowing just how much we and our children have lost.

Anne Treneer's *School House in the Wind* recalls in loving detail the experience of growing up in a Cornish village in the late Victorian period. For Anne, as for Ida, the spiritual is instinctively and naturally articulated in the language of scripture and liturgy. The companionship of the wind about her house is the friendship of God the Holy Spirit. When she hears the story of Jacob wrestling with God, she sees him struggling to open the heavy front door of their schoolhouse.

'No words have been found to relate exactly the mysterious relationship of our bodies with the air—a body breathing air in and out, and surrounded by air except where the soles of our feet touch the earth. "And he breathed into his nostrils the breath of life" comes nearest' (Treneer, 1944, 19).

Like Anne Treneer, Leo Tregenza—his *Harbour Village* is another of our Cornish Childhoods—is familiar with religious language and Biblical imagery. One Sunday he and his siblings set off for Sunday School in Mousehole. That at least is what they wish everyone to think they are doing. But the children have other plans and they head for Lamorna Cove to bathe. As they walk through the cornfields, they occasionally pluck an ear of corn and rub the grain out into their hands.

'Here we were, playing truant from Sunday School and yet we seemed to have come right into the New Testament atmosphere. Our walk had the elements of a living parable in it, our own infringement of the Law, the farmer and his fields, seedtime and harvest, and the wild flowers, the despised tares... We were crossing paths with Christ and his disciples in that other cornfield, with glimpses of some city of the Holy Land' (Tregenza, 1997, 115-116).

These children are blessed beyond most western children these days, even those who live in the country, by the freedom of the field and woods and hills. But they are blessed too by the fact that they have been immersed in a *language*, the language of faith—of scripture and liturgy—with which to speak of these things.

So far, so rural. But what of the urban child? We have already asked whether the urban is inimical to the spiritual, a possibility that must concern us now that half the world's population live in cities. But, as we have seen, it is not the case that the spirit of the child is inevitably quenched in the city.

Molly Weir grew up in the Gorbals, Glasgow's slums, now long demolished. Religion touches and lifts her spirit. She enjoys going to church. 'The atmosphere of church was soothing and mysterious, and I loved every minute of it' (Weir, 1988, 125). She loves too the annual 'tent mission'. During the mission, she makes sure that at home there are always extra Abernethy biscuits in the tin in case Jesus calls for tea—as, after all, he did for Zacchaeus. She acts out the missioner's service. When her Grannie complains about her noise she says that Jock Troup, the missioner, had told them that the streets of the New Jerusalem would be filled with the voices of little children.

These city children, like their country cousins, had been told the Gospel story, a narrative that gave them a language with which to interpret and voice their spiritual experience. This gift of language—to emphasise the point again—is the supreme service of religion to the spirit. We shall return to the all-important role of religious language in the nurture of the spirit in our next chapter.

Rosina Gow Graham—the 'Kirsty' of the memoir she wrote—was another urban child. She remembers growing up in the late Victorian period in Berwick-on-Tweed. Hers is a deeply felt, beautifully written, text and—for us—important text. Kirsty's family religion was 'a formal, faintly boring undertaking, unemotional, and predominantly Presbyterian'. But she also encounters the worship of the Salvationists and this transports her. She exults in their noisy services. In later life, she tells us, the beating of a drum will recall,

'when heaven's door swung back to let out the dawn wind; the upward flight of her heart at noon, the sands glinting, the waves' gossamer embroideries against the edge of a solid world. It all came back *in matchless unity*, the dearness of that lost coast' (Graham, 1961, 95-97).

My italics are to draw attention to the potential of religion, at least religion of the less inhibited Salvationist sort, to integrate the different aspects of the child's experience.

One aspect of the child spiritual nature is his or her dawning moral awareness. As we have seen, it is a development in which religion has done much damage. Religion, at least the Christian religion, has often had the effect—if not made it its business—of making children feel guilty. Much more could be said about the harm religion has done in this respect than the limits of this essay permit. But if religion can instil guilt, it can also, so our memoirs attest, assuage guilt and soothe the wounded spirit—even if those wounds were of religion's making.

Kirsty—to stay with her—is overwhelmed by guilt when she puts out her tongue to her mother. Desperately she wonders how she can be forgiven. How can she go direct to God, 'the vengeful ancient'? Kneeling at the washstand in her mother's room, she blurts out, 'Oh, God, take away this heart of stone and give me a heart of flesh'. She then switches to the more kindly Jesus and confesses in a tiny voice that she had put out her tongue. The burden of guilt falls from her.

"'Happy, happy Kirsty, blessed one," proclaimed the watcher over her. "I bore you on eagle's wings and brought you unto Myself'" (100-104).

Another child who knew what it was to be forgiven was 'Susan', the young Alison Uttley. She describes how she was punished for hiding in the garden to avoid helping with the housework.

'She sobbed, but when she said her prayers she asked for God's forgiveness and lay down happy. That was the best of prayers, she could sin quite a lot in the day, knowing that when she prayed she would be forgiven' (Uttley, 1936, 32).

It perhaps needs to be underlined that Kirsty and Susan, now grown-up, have not shared these memories with us for our amusement. They are not inviting us to smile with them at the naive children they once were. George MacDonald reminds us somewhere that the response of Jesus to the child who owns up to trivial misdemeanour—trivial, that is, to the morally thick-skinned adult—would not be to laugh the matter off. His word, rather, would be 'Neither do I condemn you. Go and sin no more.'

The rare spirit

We saw how Ira Gandy found her little village church companionable. A far grander building shaped the spirit of another child. John Raynor, who grew up in the precincts of Westminster Abbey and whose father was a housemaster at Westminster School, tells us that he made friends more readily with 'inanimates' than with other children. These inanimates possessed for him a life which 'put the sluggish animism of most humans in the shade'. The most dominating of those inanimate friends was the abbey itself. 'Its ubiquitous presence ensured that one never wholly forgot the ascending spiritual impulse life should be' (Raynor, 1973, 9-10).

We need to stay with the musician John Raynor. There is something Blake-like in John Raynor, the child, who sees in a vision the skeleton of a sparrow become 'a living bird before the throne of God' (76). After his death, one of his friends wrote, 'John was one of the purest artists who ever lived, one of the world's most beautiful people...Every second of the time I spent with him was fully alive and alert to the whole force of life, material and spiritual'. A reading of John Raynor's account of his childhood banishes any misgivings that such a tribute must be exaggerated.

If Raynor was a remarkable adult, he was certainly a remarkable child too. He lived in a historic house in Dean's Yard beneath the Abbey, but it was not where he grew up that made his childhood unusual. We sometimes speak of some adults as 'rare spirits'. A child can be a rare spirit too and Raynor was one. The rarity of such children, exceptionally sensitive and far-seeing and thus unusually vulnerable and prey to pain—children such as those George MacDonald and Walter de la Mare loved to write about—does not exclude them from our study. The 'abnormal child' may be the 'normative' child, 'the childlike child', the Christlike child.

One of the chapters in Raynor's *A Westminster Childhood* is entitled 'The Bright and the Dark'. Few of our memoirs testify so powerfully both to the spiritual joy and to the intense spiritual distress that the same one child can experience. We have noted in earlier chapters the exultations that blessed and the anguish that afflicted this susceptible child. In our last chapter we saw how singing compensated for the monotony of the sermons he had to sit under and we shall say more in our next chapter how the abbey spoke to this child—who was to become an accomplished composer—through its music. Here we register how a great church building can silently foster the child's spirit.

We shall return briefly to the case of 'the spiritually gifted' child—if such there be—in our concluding chapter.

Fine old Pastor Briand

As we saw with Maxim Gorky, how far a child's spiritual life is nurtured and encouraged to flourish has everything to do with the character of those who represent the things of the spirit to the child. Thank God, ministers of religion and Sunday School teachers are not always as repellent as 'the furtive she-evangelist Miss Crouch' whom we recall with a shudder. Carl Nielsen, the composer, remembers a minister who meant much to him.

'As I approached confirmation age I went to be prepared by fine old Pastor Briand...I can have heard little of what he said and probably learned nothing, for I could not take my eyes off his figure, which transported me into a more beautiful world' (Nielsen, 1953, 101).

James Kirkup records his debt to his Sunday School teachers. They were, he tells us,

'Plain, honest workmen in their good suits who spoke a language and a dialect we felt at home with. I remember the fervour of "the brethren" who spontaneously led us in prayer, and in particular the thrilling conviction of those teachers who spoke with such down-to-earth passion about the worth of prayer and the need of faith in prayer that the children in their classes were spellbound by the spiritual as well as the practical uses of "taking it to the Lord"'.
One of those teachers made a lifelong impression on him.

'(He) made me realize so vividly the personality and uniqueness of Jesus that ever after I looked upon Him as a real being, a personal friend who was with me always. Those teachers saw a vision of heaven in terms of real life' (Kirkup, 1959, 118-120).

The sensual, the seasonal and the spiritual

As we have seen, the evidence of many of our memoirs is that the impact of religion is powerfully sensual. We need to re-emphasise that at no time of life, least of all childhood, is the sensual the enemy of the spiritual. We saw how frequently our writers record how things smelled when they were small. Judging from our memoirs, it exaggerates but little to suggest that the extent to which religion nourishes the child's spirit depends on what it *smells* like. I turn again to the poet and novelist Eiluned Lewis, the 'Lucy' of her *Dew on the Grass*. As we saw in our second chapter, her memories of church-going in rural Wales at the beginning of the twentieth century are a rich register of sensual experiences.

'The inside of Pengarth church reminded Lucy of the potato house at home: they both had the same cool, earthy smell. Kneeling on a hassock that scratched her bare knees she peeped through her fingers at the disciples in the East window with their curly beards and red dressing-gowns. Glancing round at the bent heads of the congregation, she wondered excitedly whether, as God was in the midst of them, she might surprise Him by suddenly lifting the green curtain on the chancel wall' (Lewis, 1934,60).

She is distracted by the mounting storm outside. 'Lucy decided that God was no longer hiding behind the green curtains: He must be flinging the clouds across the sky' (60-62) She wriggles round to see other children in church. Eiluned Lewis obliges us to notice the sort of things, such as scratchy hassocks, that children are most likely to remember from their time in church. The fact that the context of these recollections is a world remote from our own children's world does not make those memories any less instructive.

Lucy describes how the carol-singers come to their farm. In doing so she makes the connections which adults find so hard to make. We do not have to tease out the separate threads of her train of thought—the religious, the theological, the spiritual, and the compassionate.

'When the carol-singers sing "See the tender lamb appears", Lucy is not sure whether they meant Jesus or the first forlorn little lamb that would soon be born in the winter fields. The two grew confused in her mind: she knew only that it was something young and tender which had braved the cold and hardness of the world, something which might be hurt if she did not do something to help it, if it did not wrap it safely in her arms...' They sing 'The holly and the ivy'. 'It was a sad dark tune, and now Lucy understood that nothing she could do would keep the little lamb of God from being hurt. How cold it had grown suddenly! They had all lost their way in the dark wood, and the sharp leaves of the holly were wet with blood' (Lewis, 1934, 181).

It would be a bad mistake to dismiss this remarkable passage as confused. What we have here is not confusion but fusion, the holding together of what adults put asunder, the transient suffused by the transcendent.

For Anne Treneer too, the Christmas story merges with the unfolding tale of her daily life.

'It seemed to me that everything was happening at that moment. The shepherds were on the Greeb, the baby was in a nest of Trevesan hay, and in our sky was the great light with the angels singing "Glory to God in the highest, and on earth peace, good will towards men"' (Treneer, 1944, 86).

Other high days and holy seasons are woven into the pattern of Anne Treneer's everyday life. In Lent the children imitate the troops of Midian, as they prowl around the kitchen table before swooping on a bun. Anne Treneer tells us, 'I once had a new blue frock on Trinity Sunday, but only once...My new blue frock is inextricably mingled with "Holy, holy, holy, Lord God Almighty"' (106).

God forgive us if we smile condescendingly on such children's muddled thinking, as perhaps we suppose it to be. For what these children experienced was the connectedness of liturgy and life, a sense of the sacredness of the familiar, lost—lost beyond recovery, one sometimes fears—in a world adrift. Anne Treneer writes,

'Yet though not a naturally religious child, I am glad I was taken to church regularly, initiated into the Christian faith, and helped to participate in the profound poetry of the Christian year. Though inattentive, I came insensibly to know the liturgy word for word, and to live in the double rhythm of the earthly seasons and of man's noblest imagining' (26).

The truth beyond the stars

For the present writer the most moving memoir of childhood in the English language—albeit countless such memoirs remain unread—is Percy

Lubbock's *Earlham*. Here is a radiant evocation of the spiritual and the religious at one. The memoir is a sequence of recollections of the holidays which the young Percy Lubbock spent in his grandfather's ancestral home in Earlham in Norfolk. His beloved grandfather is the owner of the great house and its estates but he is also the parish priest. Lubbock concludes his recollections with a description of a service of Evening Prayer, conducted by his grandfather in Earlham church, one Sunday in September. The boy's holiday is over and next day he must go back to school. As dusk deepens in the little church, lit only by two or three candles, the child is moved by a sense of awe—'of awe that in no way dismayed or oppressed, but rather sustained and encouraged a young spirit in its wordless answer to something larger than itself' (Lubbock, 1922, 249). Lubbock recalls his saintly grandfather's sermon.

'There was nothing in it all that a child might be supposed to understand; and a child accordingly, listening in a dream, scarcely heeding or apprehending a word, was brought without check into the mind that could worship in spirit and in truth' (250).
The child experiences a mystical awareness beyond words.
'The barriers that are about us in the world, separating soul from soul, seemed to be as nothing; and even the chasm that encircles our small humanity, that isolates it in the midst of the illimitable unknown, had vanished for an hour—freely, freely our imprisoned thought could escape to the truth beyond the stars' (252).

Lubbock's account is a surpassingly beautiful piece of writing, but its importance for us lies, not in its use of English, sublime as it is, but in how exactly it demonstrates the rightful role of religion in the service of the spirit. The religion young Percy experienced at Earlham gave him a sensory awareness of the transcendent. That awareness was validated by those dear to him, those whose love for him bespoke a love greater still. And it was expressed in a language that gave his spirit voice—even though it was a language that he had yet to fully understand. What he sensed, those he loved, and the language they spoke—provided a threefold nourishment of his spirit. So the child Percy Lubbock received these three gifts: sensory sacraments of the spiritual, the love of others that channelled the love of another, and a language which one day would allow him to speak of these things and which will bring him at last to a place where words are left behind.

But we cannot leave those words behind just yet. We stay with words—and with the music that accompanies them—in our next chapter.

CHAPTER 9

WORÒS ANÒ ᴄᴏUSIC

W e have wondered whether the children we have met are typical. As we would expect of writers, many of them remember from a young age being moved by the sound of words. Are we to suppose that these children had a better ear for words than those whose business in later life was less bookish? No doubt those who end up as writers are likely to have always enjoyed the rhythms and resonances of language. But we can be sure that far more children are born with an ear for words than the few who later write about their childhoods. Perhaps what distinguishes our writers is simply that they were lucky enough to hear beautiful words well used. Sadly, that blessing is denied to many children today.

We have emphasised the importance of a fitting language for life and growth in spirit. This will be both a language which the spirit can apprehend long before it is understood conceptually and a language in which the child's own spirit can begin to find voice. The aim of this chapter is to illustrate from our memoirs how language serves the growing spirit. We shall notice how the very sound of words can enchant our children and then, as those words begin to fall in step, how the power of story can strengthen the spirit. More must then be said about the spiritually formative potential of scriptural language and narrative and about the nurture of the spirit by the languages of music and liturgy.

The spirit sustained by word and story

Little children love words, relishing the sound of them without worrying about what they mean. Nonsense or near-nonsense can captivate them. Children delight in the drumbeat of powerful rhythms, revelling, for example, in the popular Dr Seuss books, *The Cat in the Hat* and the rest.

They demand that their favourite songs and rhymes be repeated over and over again. The taste for the liturgical, with its rhythms and repetitions, has deep roots.

Paul Vaughan, growing up in the 30s in south London, was close to his brother David, his senior by seventeen months. The two small boys enjoy making up words for people and for things that lacked names of their own. The girl who operated the lift in the department store was a *demnity-fess*. Figures decorating the icing on a Christmas cake were *sallagy-savies*. A long face with mouth ajar was a *goggox* face (Vaughan, 1994, 44).

Loftier language too can mesmerize children long before it means much. Konstantin Paustovsky's Aunt Nadya takes her nephew to visit her friend Lisa. That evening they drive through a park that the poet Pushkin liked to walk in. Befitting the time and place, Lisa recites a poem by Pushkin. Paustovsky comments,

'I could not understand all of it, but the power and music of the poetry, the evening light on the park, the ancient lime-trees and the clouds drifting above them, all combined to put me in a magical mood, and the whole of this day has remained in my memory as a quiet celebration of spring' (Paustovsky, 1964, 42).

Young Konstantin loves stories too and his grandfather is a fund of them. 'It was partly to my grandfather,' he claimed, 'that I owed the romanticism and the susceptibility to new impressions which turned my childhood into a succession of collisions with reality' (20). Joy in stories is evident in all our Russian memoirs of childhood. Serghei Aksakoff is enthralled by *The Arabian Nights*. 'What, then,' he asks 'is the secret of the spell they laid on me? I believe it is to be found in that passion for marvellous innate, more or less, in all children and was less repressed by sober sense in my case than in most' (241). Maxim Gorky is enchanted by his grandmother's stories. 'She told her tales in a quiet, mysterious voice, her face close to mine, gazing into my eyes with dilated pupils as though she were pouring into my heart a stream of strength to support me' (Gorky, 1961,13).

Each of these three recollections of Russian childhoods testifies to the spiritually formative potential of stories. Stories cause 'collisions with reality'. They expose the insufficiency of the ordinary account of things to explain the totality of experience, obliging us to reconsider what is real and what is not. The failure of 'sober sense' to satisfy the child's innate passion for the marvellous suggests that more than sobriety and common-sense is needed to explain things. Stories in which the child can imaginatively engage can become 'a stream of strength', nourishing the child's being at levels deeper than any assertions or propositions, however edifying, can reach.

The spirit sustained by scripture.

Many of our childhoods were spent where the Bible was still read. There is much evidence in memories of those childhoods of the power of Biblical language and Biblical stories to shape and nourish the child's spirit. The children's writer Lucy Boston remembers her first day at school. The second lesson that day was 'Reading'. She remembers that the passage she was given to read was the twelfth chapter of Ecclesiastes: 'Remember now thy Creator in the days of thy youth while the evil days come not.' She describes how this passage was 'stuttered and stammered over round the class with reluctance.' She adds, 'I had of course heard it before, but it seemed to me now a revelation and a glory in words' (Boston, 1979, 33-34). She shares her passion for poetry with her friend Connie. If her class was asked to memorise a famous passage, she and Connie 'would have privately learned half the book simply for pleasure'. She tells us that she learned great parts of the Authorised Version of the Bible by heart (49-50).

Words shape us before they are understood. Biblical language, that will make sense only much later, already feeds the growing spirit. Eiluned Lewis lies in a hammock under the sycamore tree. She repeats wonderful words that she has heard for the first time that morning,

'"To be carnally minded is death; but to be spiritually minded is life and peace." "Carnally minded, carnally minded," she murmured. What proud, glowing words they were! She saw them as high-stepping, processional horses, caparisoned in scarlet' (Lewis, 1934, 31).

Elizabeth Hamilton, growing up in a spacious home in Ireland, was moved by the sound of the psalms which 'rang out with a cheerful lilt, verse leaping after verse like goats upon the mountains' (Hamilton, 1963, 123). Molly Weir, child of 'the Gorbals', Glasgow's noxious slums, loved the language of the Bible. Needless to say, the version she grew to love was that of the 'King James Bible'. She writes,

'I loved (the Bible's) rolling phrases, and used to race along to school chanting "Tell it not in Gath, publish it not in the streets of Askelon, lest the daughters of the Philistines rejoice, lest the daughters of the uncircumcised triumph." And as I turned the corner, I wailed, "Ye daughters of Israel, weep over Saul, who clothed you in scarlet and other delights, who put ornaments of gold upon your apparel..." What marvellous sounds they were!'

To be sure, she still cheerfully sings the rude playground songs, but, she tells us, 'they were just daft rhyming sounds, but ah, the language of the Holy Bible was quite different and stirred me to the heart' (Hamilton, 1963, 248-249).

William Magan, who, as we saw, found the Irish Episcopal church of his boyhood boring, nevertheless 'loved the Bible and Bible stories'. 'Who could ever forget a phrase such as "And David lamented with this lamentation over Saul and Jonathan his son"?' Images of biblical characters remained vividly in his mind—Elisha turning the she-bears on the mocking children; the palms of Jezebel's hands after the dogs had eaten her; 'poor Ruth', and many more.

He is taught the Lord's Prayer, the Catechism, and the Ten Commandments by his mother.

'Much of it I did not understand, as was doubtless the case with my mother herself. The meaning, however, was the least important part of it to her. What mattered was submitting to a stern piece of religious discipline. Some splendid passages did excite my imagination. 'To renounce the devil and all his works,' in the Catechism. That was a grand resounding phrase' (Magan, 1996, 98-102).

The Jewish child John Gross was fascinated by the language of Biblical stories long before, as he puts it, 'the stories and the language in which they had been written came together'. His fancy, he tells us, was caught by such glorious names as 'Abana' and 'Pharpar'. For him the characters in the Bible stories, 'were not merely as real to me as Ali Baba or Robin Hood, they were *really* real—all this had once taken place—and they were the more real for my feeling personally linked to them: they were the founders of the family'. His engagement with the old stories is made the more intense by his hearing them in Hebrew. '*Ha-shomayim*...came to seem the thing itself, and the English translation "heaven" no more than a pale approximation'. Some stories, however, do disturb him. The account of Abraham's readiness to sacrifice Isaac raises doubts in his mind about 'what kind of God is it who commanded a father to kill his son' (Gross, 2001, 17-18).

Helen Forrester, growing up in a Liverpool slum, falls into conversation with an elderly scholarly stranger. She tells him her reason for no longer going to church. 'We are so dirty; we cannot afford soap'. But in recalling this conversation she remembers too that she had loved going to church on those rare occasions she did. She had loved church for 'its wealth of beauty', not least for the language of the King James Bible, the prayer-book, and the hymns (Forrester, 1974, 161-166).

Nancy Thompson grew up in Middlesborough in the early twentieth century. Her childhood was as poor as Helen Forrester's, but for her too the Bible was enriching. Her grandfather reads her the story of Balaam's ass.

'As he read I grew more and more excited. The whole of it was wonderful beyond any story I had heard. Wonderful that the ass could see the angel while the man could not; wonderful that the ass was a SHE' (Nancy Thomson, 1986, 12).

We saw how Richard Church's mother gave him a Bible on his seventh birthday and that he began his reading of the Bible with the book of Job, a text not normally commended to seven-year-olds. The little boy found Job intoxicating. 'It acted on my seven-year brain,' Church tells us, 'as a lashing of ship's rum would have acted on my stomach. I mouthed the wonderful phrases to myself, rolling them round and round, growing daily more word-drunk.' His mother suggests 'he ought to think more about what the Bible was about and not in the way it was written' (Church, 1955, 81-82).

The children at James Kirkup's school were made to chant together long passages from the Bible.

> 'I loved the Bible for its thin, print-packed pages sizzling with italics, for its wonderful stories of Joseph, Daniel, David and Jonathan, and for the person of Jesus: to me they were real people, and the events they took part in did not surprise me' (Kirkup, 1959, 86-87).

Some of our writers stress the formative power of scriptural stories, while insisting that the power of the story did not depend on its correspondence to anything that actually happened or on a theistic account of things. The musician Francesca Allinson grew up on the outer reaches of Bloomsbury. She and her brother were brought up as 'free-thinkers, allowed to question and doubt every religious belief' (Allinson, 1937, 39). 'As the habit of disbelief was not really ingrained in me,' we read, 'my assent was to be had for any stirring belief and I was open to every wind that blew'. Francesca's friend Thea tells her the story of Adam and Eve.

> 'She described the Fall as a lovers' parting: there was God, great and yet aching, impotent for all his Godhead to beget love except on the same terms as mortals, buying it as dearly as they...The story, whether its events had actually taken place or not, bore within it its own truth of existence' (59).

Such stories are 'truth-bearing', the adult Allinson claims, whether or not they relate to what happened, whether or not their theistic framework is to be understood in realist terms. To try to defend that claim would be to take us into theological and philosophical waters too turbulent to navigate here. Here I simply note what emerges so powerfully from memoirs of childhoods spent in a world where Bible stories were known and loved— that scriptural language and narrative are spiritually formative.

The stories are thrilling but so too was the language in which they were once told. In our contemporary anxiety to render the text of the Bible into a language which is readily intelligible—an anxiety amounting to paranoia, so addictive is the compulsion to produce ever more translations—we have forgotten that the intelligibility of sacred texts is not all that matters about them, certainly not to small children. We have seen how important the *feel* of a Bible was to children we have met. So too, as we have now seen, was the *sound* of it. Sense is not served by disregard of the senses.

The spirit sustained by music.

Children are moved by the sound of words. So too are they by music, whether secular or religious, as many memoirs testify. Music arrests attention and captures the spirit. Even as a tiny child, Bryan Magee was brought to a standstill whatever he was doing whenever he hears strains of music—whether from a beggar or a band.

'I would sometimes stand stock still, rooted to the spot, gazing at the source of the music and completely lost in my own attention to it, and would then refuse to move and have to be dragged away' (Magee, 2003, 212).

When lullabies are sung, as once they were in the west and as they still are in many cultures, music gently sends the children to sleep. Elisaveta Fen recalls a lullaby sung by her nurse:

'Sleep, my child, go to sleep
Be thy sleep sweet and deep...
I have hired nurses three
To watch all night o'er thee.'

The three guardians are the eagle and the sun, and the wind, but it is the wind that is most steadfast. The wind tells its mother,

'I haven't touched the golden stars,
Nor chased the waves across the bars,
I had a child in my keep,
And rocked its cradle and made it sleep."

Elisaveta comments, 'To be given the wind, the eagle, and the sun as nurses made me feel a very special child, a royal or divine child. (But) it was the devotion of the wind which filled me with proud delight.' (Fen, 1961, 52-53)

We are not surprised to learn that many of our writers enjoyed lively music by day or fell asleep to quieter music at bedtime. Less to have been expected, perhaps, is how many of them as children were moved to sadness by the music they heard. We know as adults the melancholy that music has power to evoke. The evidence of our memoirs is that this sadness is not a rarefied sentiment which only grown-ups experience—which, indeed, they may set out to cultivate and indulge. Children know the same haunting sadness when they hear some kinds of music and, as our memoirs show, they are no more able to explain it than adults are.

Maxim Gorky's Uncle Yakov's sings to his guitar. His music 'demanded utter silence; it rushed like a rivulet from somewhere far away, seeped through walls and floors and stirred the heart, awakening a strange, sad, restless feeling' (Gorky, 1961, 46).

Konstantin Paustovsky remembers how his grandfather used to tell stories and sing 'in his quavering voice' the songs of the ox-cart drivers and of the Cossacks.

'I liked the ox-cart drivers' songs for their nostalgic monotony. They were songs you could sing for hours on end to the creaking of the cart-wheels as you lay on your cart, looking at the sky. The Cossack songs evoked an obscure sadness in me' (Paustovsky, 1964, 16-17).

The music of the band playing in the park moves James Kirkup. So too do the chiming of the town clock, the murmur of the sea, and 'the nostalgic waltzes of my mother's girlhood'. These 'made my heart ache for her, and for the passing of time...They were all laughter, gaiety, remorse, regret, those tunes, and my heart was always filled with a bitter-sweet pang when I heard my mother faintly humming them' (Kirkup, 1957, 117).

The blind Egyptian boy, Shusha Guppy, is moved by his father's singing.

'Of all musical instruments the human voice is the most beautiful, for it is made by God. My father had a beautiful voice, a deep mellow baritone with an exceptionally rich and velvety timbre. As a child, I would sometimes wake up in the night and hear him chanting the Quran and the midnight prayer in his study... I sometimes cried, which brought Nanny with soothing words. It seems to me that I have searched for that enchantment in every beautiful voice ever since' (Guppy, 1988, 148-149).

Francesca Allinson, who herself became an accomplished musician, remembers how music—for all its beauty, because of its beauty—could be the source of distress. From time to time she stayed with her uncle Robert, a string-player, who would sometimes of an evening form a quartet from his friends. His niece, upstairs in bed, would lie awake listening. '*Weltschmerz* swam about me and into me, and then hugging me tighter and tighter became a particular sorrow; supposing my mother should die?' (Allinson, 1937, 74)

Like Francesca Allinson, John Raynor, who deservedly has claimed much of our attention in this study, grew up to be a musician. Indeed it sounds as if he was born to be a musician and so it is hardly surprising that the music of Westminster Abbey moved him as it did. Raynor was only four years old, he tells us, when for the first-time 'the Abbey had spoken to me directly'. He hears the gradually rising and increasingly thrilling sound of the Abbey's great organ. 'It seemed that very heart of the pain and the beauty was exposed' and the little boy bursts into 'wild tears, half of excitement and half of fear'. We note that element of fear. The awakened spirit, as Wordsworth taught us, has reason to be afraid (Raynor, 1973, 10-11).

Towards the end of his memoir, Raynor speaks of the abbey's organ as a 'tree of music...whose roots were deep in the earth and whose branches broke through the fan-vaulted roof until they touch the ceiling of heaven' (210).

Raynor is moved in spirit by singing, both sacred and secular. He is moved to rapture by the beauty of a choirboy's singing. 'I stood as in a dream, drinking in the blend of candlelit boy and a moment in time' (14). But he is delighted too by the sound of the street barrel-organ.

'As the penultimate phrase, "She is my Lily of Laguna", soared, hovering, before closing its wings and gently falling to earth, it seemed that my whole being, exposed, extended itself in trembling ecstasy, towards whatever was the real source of the music' (120).

John Raynor comes to love hymns and to sense their truth while still a small child. Some hymns, however, disturb him. A verse such as 'But the evening cometh on/ And the dark, cold night' speaks to him of looming peril. 'Even while we were singing it,' he recalls, 'the air would grow thin and the darkness of spiritual distress and fear hover in the room' (50).

Many of our children, like John Raynor, are moved by the hymns they sing and sometimes, like him, they catch a sense of what these hymns are saying long before they can say what they mean. James Kirkup recalls how the language of hymns touched him deeply. His unhappiness at school is taken up and given a voice in the hymn they sing at the end of the day.

> 'Now the day is over,
> Night is drawing nigh
> Shadows of the evening
> Steal across the sky.'

Kirkup writes,

'That sad little tune, with its haunting simplicity, would move me every time I heard it...My heart would ache with the poignancy of the words. And once again I would catch glimpses of the spirit-world, and knew better than ever what ghosts and dying mean' (Kirkup, 1957, 124).

On a Sunday School parade they sing the hymn, 'There is a green hill far away'. Kirkup writes,

'I could understand only imperfectly what these words meant, but I sensed completely their sad acceptance, and their tragedy: they sent cold shivers down my spine, and blurred my eyes with tears (154).

The child's eyes blur with tears. There is remarkable similarity and consistency in the terms our adult authors use to describe the mood into which music—and words set to music—put them. One speaks of 'a strange, sad, restless feeling', another of 'an obscure sadness', another of a heart filled with 'a bitter-sweet pang', yet another of the *Weltschmerz* music can induce. A Persian boy cries to hear his father chant from the Quran; a little girl listens to a string quartet and wonders whether her mother will die. John Raynor, who will himself become a composer as well as a fine writer, suffers 'spiritual distress and fear' when, in the abbey, they sing of the onset of 'the dark, cold night'.

What is happening here? Why should some music and certain hymns make some young children so very sad? Don Haworth is one of the most entertaining of our writers and the least likely to be accused of morbid melancholy. Yet it is a comment of Howarth which perhaps best explains why such music has the effect it does.

Don Haworth grew up in Lancashire, where he went to a Methodist Sunday School. The teaching does nothing for him except to furnish his memory—and to entertain us—with the recollection of a dim young lady who read word-for-word from the teachers' hand-book. So the children hear the teacher intone, 'A certain man went down from Jerusalem to Jericho...Explain to the children the hardship of a journey before trams and buses', and so on—'Go and do thou likewise. Methodist Publications, 4d. post-free'—to the end of the lesson.

The simple hymns they sang meant much more to Don.

'We sang without attention, but sometimes the words gave a glimpse of an undiscovered country and filled us with a sweet sense of loss for what we had never known' (Haworth, 1986, 119-120).

There is a delicate lightness of touch in Haworth's memoir but deep discernment too. As he sang the child glimpsed 'another country' and was filled with the 'sense of loss'. There awakes in the child a perception of what Forrest Reid—and A. L. Rowse and Kathleen Raine with him —saw as the fundamental truth of the human condition, that we are all far from home. Music and words set to music can pierce the carapace we use to block out consciousness of our spiritual plight, the truth that we are all exiles but do not know where to look for the land we have lost.

Nancy Thompson tells us why one hymn sung in her chapel meant so much to her. Her recollection is one of the most telling examples in our literature of the potential of language and music to nourish the child's spirit .

> 'Even then I had the words of many hymns by heart. Their sound was woven through the substance of my life and was to me as the sound of lullabies to other children. I absorbed and retained them easily...But this was the hymn with the meaning. It did something to me. It picked me up and carried me to another place and held me there, light and comfortable and still as if at the centre of a great ball.
>> "Day is dying in the west,
>> Heaven is touching earth with rest..."
> The sensation was so hard to define that as it recurred and forced me to recognise its existence, thus claiming a place in language, I came gradually to name it as the "homelike feeling". When it gathered me up, all alien and harsh sensations were removed and I was suspended in an atmosphere where all was well. The experience had its opposite which I thought of as "unhomelike", and either would envelop me suddenly without apparent cause' (Nancy Thompson, 1986, 3-4).

On one occasion a hymn Nancy is asked to sing proves transporting —to use the only fitting term. Her head teacher asks her to stand at the front of her infant class and sing 'Jesus high in glory, lend a listening ear'. Nancy stumbles at her first attempt to sing the hymn, but her head teacher plays over the introduction again and she begins afresh.

> 'Then I left the classroom for that place where things were acutely real and as they should be. I took a breath and was ready to begin' (22).

I have already referred to Percy Lubbock's *Earlham*, his radiant account of holidays spent in his Norfolk family home—and surely a masterpiece. Some years later, in his *Shades of Eton*, Lubbock wrote too about his term-times at school. Those schooldays are not depicted as a dark contrast to the blissful holidays he had portrayed so evocatively in the earlier work. Far from it. The gift of happiness, nourished by his family, did not fail him at school, even though life at Eton in the nineteenth century must often have been harsh. But Lubbock's *Shades of Eton* is not just about that famous place. Before Eton there was his little preparatory school. One memory of those earliest schooldays speaks of the revelatory power of music.. The boys are gathered in the Headmaster's drawing room—a treat before bedtime— to listen to the Head's daughter playing her violin. Lubbock writes,

> 'Presently, unawares, I was floating, flying, soaring, loose from the world, borne aloft in liberation, in a warmth of glory—seeing and feeling and knowing with a strange clarity—knowing everything, but by a revelation direct not in words. So it went on, for an immense lapse of time; and then at last it hovered and sank and came to an end—a sudden end, leaving me still in the air for an almost painful drop to the earth, by myself, some moments after it had ceased' (Lubbock, 1929, 60).

We weigh these words. 'With a strange clarity', the child saw and felt and knew. What did he know? What had been revealed to him?
Everything.

The spirit sustained by liturgy

Margery Hicks was the child of parents who were devout but who found it hard to settle religiously. Eventually they joined a Christian Science meeting. Before their move to Christian Science, the family went to the Bristol City Road Methodist Church. 'There had been a pitchpine ugliness at City Road,' she tells us, 'that even at the age of five I had found aesthetically distressing.'

Fortunately she still remembered the kindergarten of the Church of England school she had attended when she was even younger. The Anglican prayers she learned in that kindergarten sustained her long after she had left it.

'Besides, the Church (of England) had already laid a finger on me. For at school even the kindergarten attended the morning prayers of assembly and the evening prayers of dismissal. "*Lord now lettest thou thy servant depart in peace according to thy word.*" The words were a silvery beam of light that penetrated the Hall and beyond into the smelly cloakroom where shortly I must engage in the scuffle for hats and boots; and was not entirely dispersed even there' (Hicks, 1969, 69).

Some of our writers record their abiding gratitude for a religious upbringing and for liturgy's enrichment of their lives long after they have ceased to believe that religious claims are true. The Cornishman A. L. Rowse writes,

'When I think of my life as a whole, I do not in the end think of myself, but of the sum of those moments of ecstasy which is my real inner life. They constitute my revealed religion—a revelation of the world as beauty...Religion meant nothing to me intellectually' (Rowse, 1942, 154).

Although religion meant nothing to Rowse the intellectual, the church's influence on him at 'the aesthetic and the emotional' level remained profound and lifelong. He is eternally grateful for his grounding in the Book of Common Prayer. 'How can one ever forget such language, once it has been so implanted in the ear? (143) The beauty of its liturgy drew Rowse to Anglo-Catholicism. 'I am a High Church unbeliever,' he tells us (154-158). All his adult life he remains painfully torn between his intellectual repudiation of religious claims and, as he puts it, the 'emotional sympathies and the strong bias of his early life' (164-165).

Can words still burn?

When Kevin Crossley-Holland was a boy his father showed him 'Traherne's burning words' about the cornfields, the 'orient and immortal wheat' of childhood. 'Although I didn't fully comprehend them, these words scorched me,' he writes. 'They branded me. I knew then that there are truths deeper than logic or understanding, deeper than words, and my father knew that I knew' (Crossley-Holland, 2009, 32-33).

Crossley-Holland uses fiery imagery to convey just how intensely, deeply, and lastingly he was marked by Traherne's language. The writers we have listened to in this chapter would surely echo his talk of 'burning', 'scorching', and 'branding' to describe the impact on them of the words they heard as children. But most of those we have heard learned a language that, in their childhood, was still spoken, the language of the King James Bible and the Book of Common Prayer. That memorable language, if not quite dead, is now rarely heard and even children from church-going families will be unfamiliar with it. Instead, the scriptures and prayers they hear will be in any one—and probably in many more than one—of the countless tongues, colloquial but wholly forgettable, of contemporary worship. Similarly, their experience of music will not be of hallowed hymnody but of melodies which, however catchy, are meretricious and evanescent.

Perhaps the greatest task for a church wishing to nurture its children spiritually is to recover a common language, a language that once learned will not immediately be forgotten and which will enable them to meet and make sense of the demands made on them as human beings in a world astray. The lesson our writers teach us is that the sound of that language—as in any language a child learns—is initially as important as the sense of its words. Words mean something long before we can say what they mean. Why else does a mother talk to her child?

Perhaps the reintroduction of the Authorised Version of the Bible and the reinstatement of the Prayer Book is a lost cause. Indeed such a recovery effort may not be a wholly good cause. But the need for a language—for a single language, not a Babel of a thousand tongues—remains. The implication of the memories we have canvassed is that our children need words whose sounds are already sacramental of truths that perhaps only later will make conceptual sense.

Much emerging from this chapter, as from our earlier chapters, underlines the significance and importance of the approach to spiritual formation and Christian nurture known as Godly Play. The purpose of Godly Play is—to quote Jerome Berryman, who over half a century has developed this approach—'to help children to become native speakers of

Christian as a second language'. Jerome adds, 'I am still curious why the importance of this isn't obvious to everyone'.

We are searching our memoirs for what they imply about the nurture of the child's spirit. Much in these last pages has taught us how imperative it is that, with children, we watch our words. But we reflect on these memories too because the experience of these children challenges and instructs our own discipleship. In this chapter we have met children who glimpsed—and some who approached closely—'that place where things are acutely real and as they should be.' Our testimonies are of words and music speaking to children of 'a country far beyond the skies'—a country to which some children are brought very near. There is a telling resonance here with memories we have already touched on—with children's perceptions of 'another world' which we explored in Chapter Three and with the exultant 'peak experiences' of childhood discussed in Chapter Six.

Such children rebuke our spiritual short-sightedness. For good reason, so we persuade ourselves, our priorities are with the here and now. But our priorities have become preoccupations. Far-sighted children, such as those we have met, remind us of what we have chosen to forget, that the goal of the spiritual life is always beyond. Of course recovery of that 'original vision' does not come without cost. We will have to take to painful hearts that it is a long way home. All the more important that we do not stop singing.

CHAPTER 10

`pLAYING WITH ICONS'

F ar more memoirs of childhood have been published than it has been possible to discuss in this exploratory study. Richard Coe's *When the Grass was Taller*, published in 1984, was based on a close reading of more than six hundred of them. Countless more have been appeared since then. The temptation is to read more and more of them, for the material is ceaselessly fascinating. But that urge must be resisted and an attempt now be made to draw some conclusions.

Many memories discussed in this essay have been of childhoods lived in worlds gone by. Some of our memoirs were published a long time ago and of course they look back farther still. Now that we are well into the twenty-first century we may well question the value of conclusions drawn from such remote sources. Many children today, at least in the global north, live in worlds so different from those briefly glimpsed in these pages that we wonder what lessons such distant life-stories can hold for present day children and their spiritual nurture.

The lineaments of contemporary childhood—rich material for sociologists of childhood—are too complex and extensive to explore here. But some of the differences between yesterday's and today's children are obvious enough.

Today's children are the offspring of a technological revolution. The games they choose are on screens. They are far less frequently out of doors than earlier generations of children. Many do not experience kinship with nature because nature is a companion they never meet. They do not roam the hills and woods, whether alone or with other children. As soon as they go to school they become the victims of an ideologically determined educational programme that prioritises the delivery to them of information and marketable skills over the exploration of the imaginative, the creative, and the spiritual. They are the victims too of commercial exploitation, targeted by industries interested in children only as a lucrative market.

Childhood in the west has been commodified—and, arguably, sexualised as children at increasingly earlier ages are provided with sexual information and exposed to sexual material. Knowledge, known too soon, has made children all too knowing. And most children have grown up in a culture that has taken leave of God.

But these contemporary children—the grandchildren who share the flat where I write and their peers—are not so far removed in spirit from those we have met in these pages as to render the experience of the latter irrelevant. Were yesterday's children and today's to come face-to-face, as they do from time to time in children's stories (Helen Cresswell's marvellous *A Game of Chance* comes to mind), they would recognise each other as kindred. Evolution has not accelerated at such an exponential pace as to alter who we are, whether adults or children. If there are aspects of the experience of children of an earlier generation which contrast favourably with those of our children—their liberty to 'play out' by themselves, for example—that contrast is as alarming as it is precisely because we recognise that essentially the nature and needs of childhood are the same in our day as in our grandparents' day.

And it is not all bad. For example, for all its hidden perils, the contemporary digital culture to which our children belong—is not necessarily spiritually deleterious. Karen-Marie Yust has recently gone so far as to claim that such a culture can 'function as a spiritually enriching force' (Yust, 2014, 133-143).

Above all, the tremendous words of Jesus of Nazareth about things hidden from adults, so sure of their superior wisdom and intelligence, but revealed to infants are an abiding affirmation of the spiritual life of the child as child, 'the child as such', not only of the child born and brought up in cultures more suited, we might wistfully suppose, for his or her spiritual wellbeing.

I would argue that the continuities between the lives of the children we have met in this study and the lives of contemporary children are more significant than the discontinuities, notable as the latter are. In that conviction I look back on the recollections we have considered and ask what, in summary, we have learned from them.

Late in the day and somewhat mischievously, I mention one memoir of childhood that may not be considered a memoir at all, not least because it is only half a sentence long. Indeed many commentators tell us that it has nothing to do with childhood at all. In the course of a letter he is writing to the Christians in Rome, St Paul says 'I was alive once,' (Romans 7.9). Of course Paul, the way he does, says a lot more. Paul writes, 'I was alive once apart from the law, but when the commandment came, sin revived and I died'. And the complicated argument, which need not detain us, goes on much longer.

I stay with those first few words—'I was alive once'—and I make three audacious assertions about them: first, that Paul is talking about himself, secondly that he is talking about his own childhood, and thirdly that he is claiming that, as a child, he was—as he puts it earlier in Romans— 'alive to God in Christ Jesus' (Romans 6.11). In other words, we must give to Paul's statement 'I was alive' the great and glorious weight that the vocabulary of life carries throughout the letter to the Romans and, for that matter, throughout the New Testament. (I have defended these assertions elsewhere (*Faith and Thought*, April 2013, 13-20)).

The plain sense of what Paul says can be evaded only on the premise that a child's life is inherently defective, that the child is to be defined only by what he or she lacks. Alas, that premise is the unexamined assumption of most New Testament critics, who insist that Paul must have meant less than he said. It is also the presupposition of numerous uncomprehending adults some of whom we have met in our memoirs.

The starting point of this study has been the Pauline premise that the spiritual life is not reserved for adults. Life of the spirit is not some lofty plateau to which only grown-ups can ascend. 'Every age, every station in life,' wrote Rousseau, 'has a perfection, a ripeness, of its own' (*Rousseau*, 1911, 122). As early as the second century of the Christian era, Irenaeus had said, 'Christ therefore passed through every age, thus becoming an infant for infants, thus sanctifying infants, a child for children, thus sanctifying those who are of this age' (*Against Heresies* II, xxii, 4). We are not kettles on a conveyor belt, only complete when the last widget is in place. At no point, whether physically or spiritually, is the child an unfinished product.

The claim that we are 'born spiritual', however, does not mean that that innate spiritually flourishes equally in every child. Material impoverishment, hunger, and debilitating illness can stifle the spirit, although that need not be so. We have met many children in this study who are strong in spirit despite material deprivation. At the same time some children who never go without can seem quite unaware of 'the other and the beyond'. We remember Frances Donaldson whose childhood, she recalled, was 'without any interior life'. Having too much, it would seem, can be as threatening to the child's spiritual life as having too little.

But perhaps the reason why some children seem exceptionally spiritually sensitive is simpler. Spirituality, it appears, is a capacity, like any other inborn faculty, stronger in some children than in others. Many memoirs of childhood focus more on the child's world than on the child. The authors of these memoirs are looking around rather than looking inward or beyond. The stories they tell us certainly make intriguing social history. But we are bound to wonder, however reluctantly, whether some of these writers had much more of an interior life as children than Frances Donaldson. Our spirituality is innate. That fact, such is the evidence, is incontestable. Nevertheless our memoirs do suggest that some children are 'spirituality gifted', just as some children are gifted in, say, mathematics or music. Some children may indeed see further. There is, it seems, as we suggested in our opening chapter, a continuum of spiritual awareness. If so, Frances Donaldson and Rabindranath Tagore are at its opposite ends.

That caveat sounded, we try now to draw some threads together. Here I underline again what I said at the start, that this essay is as much a reminder of what we may have forgotten as an account of new discoveries. I simply hope that our writers—men and women who are good at writing as well as remembering—will have helped us to feel afresh what it is to be a child and to take to heart what previously we may have only acknowledged in theory. As we come to a close I will try to underline those aspects of the child's spiritual life, as recollected by our adult writers, which have impressed me most powerfully, truths about the inner life of children which I ignore at my peril—and theirs.

So what have we learned? First, however 'spiritually gifted' some children may be, the source of their primary experience of the spiritual in their earliest years, as for all other children, will be the sensory (Chapter Two).

The sensory is primary. It is not labouring the point to reiterate the implications of this first principle. We must do so because we are not yet free in the Christian west of the baleful notion that promoting the spiritual means demoting the sensual. No heresy is more harmful to the child's spiritual well-being. It really does matter both that we provide for our children 'wonderful things'—*thaumasia*—that delight the senses and that we recognise and affirm the *thaumasia* children find for themselves. The sentiment 'nothing in my hands I bring' does not express the spirit in which little children come to Jesus.

I return once more to the words with which Frank Kendon embarked on his quest, recorded in his *The Small Years*, to make sense of childhood— to 'wrestle with the angel of childhood', as he so memorably described that task.

'That which from the beginning, which we have heard, which we have seen with our eyes, which we have looked upon, and our hands have handled of the word of life. For the life was manifested, and we have seen it, and bear witness' (1 John 1.1).

It is by the things they see, hear, and handle—and by the things they taste and smell—that children grow in spirit. The small children we have met in these pages are materialist. Their spirituality is experienced as a dimension of the material, not in detachment from the material. To repeat our spiritual heath warning, about the most unhelpful instruction to give a child is the rubric telling him or her to pray with 'hands together, eyes closed'.

The primary importance of the sensory as a means of grace is demonstrated above all in the young child's experience of play. Much more might have been said in this essay about the *playing* child, but, so fundamental is play to condition of childhood, that play as a distinct theme is little explored in our memoirs. The Hoxton child Bryan Magee is one of the few of our writers to dwell on its significance.

'In my own childhood the sense of the marvellousness of things which to some extent I felt about everything was at its deepest and most intense when I was playing. I was at one with myself then, fulfilled; I was being, full out, engaged with heart and mind, full stretch, in a way I never wholly was at any other time' (Magee, 2003, 186).

The first importance of play for the flourishing of the child's spirit could hardly be more powerfully expressed. We notice that the adult, looking back, locates and anchors the child's experience of play in 'the marvellousness of *things*'. Magee's testimony,—and it is one of the most telling recollections in our memoirs—is to the sacramental significance of *thaumasia*.

I return briefly to *Sunset before Seven* in which Charles Higgins (writing under the pseudonym of Ian Dall) describes his Argentinean childhood. The little boy likes playing marbles. 'I do not think that the game of marbles has been truly appreciated by the world,' he says. The marbles themselves enchant the boy.

> 'I sat down among the long grass and looked at the marbles one by one, or let each one drop and trickle a short way through the dust...Gazing at their roundness, at the stains and stripes of colour imprisoned in the bottle-glass, I felt a keen secret pleasure which made me a little dazed and sleepy, and left behind a glow of content for some moments after I had put them in the bag' (Dall, 1936, 32-33).

We saw earlier how this child is sent away to an appalling boarding school where he is cruelly bullied. An older boy systematically smashes his precious marbles. In a moment we must revisit what we have called 'the spiritual distress' of childhood', but not before we have noticed how for this one small boy marbles are a means of grace.

Our children reach for 'the other and the beyond'. We have seen—here is a second theme of our memoirs—how the relationships children forge will often be with imaginary worlds or imaginary friends (Chapter Three). If their 'relational awareness' is not experienced in the actual relationships of their everyday lives, they will frequently find adventures just as exciting and companionship just as real in these other worlds and with these other friends.

Children have the freedom of imaginary worlds of their own making. They also make friends with, and are befriended by, imaginary companions. Our study has demonstrated how real to the child those invented worlds and unseen friends can be. For example, we saw that, for the young Richard Church, that imagined companion was Jesus.

A line of thought beckons here, even if it cannot be pursued now. Adults of pious persuasion, who will be pleased to learn of a child's friendship with Jesus, will perhaps be less approving of the friendship a child finds with the hero or heroine of a school-story—or, for that matter, some other companion of their own making. Such misgivings underestimate the capacity of Jesus Christ to change his name and appearance. Jesus of Nazareth, as we no longer sing, is indeed the 'friend of little children', but those children do not have to know him under that name to enjoy his companionship. We recall the children befriended by a lion called Aslan.

Returning to childhood can be a journey into dark places. We picture little Charles weeping over his smashed marbles. Again we pray with John Masefield, 'Lord, give to men who are old and tougher/ The things that little children suffer'. The depth and intensity of 'spiritual distress' in childhood—a third theme of this study, discussed in Chapter Four—was not anticipated in embarking on this project. A conclusion emerging as strongly as any other from our memoirs is that *children hurt* and hurt more acutely than most of us adults appreciate, unless, that is, we have the courage to revisit the darkness of our own early days and nights—those nights especially.

The child we have met on many pages of our memoirs has been 'the child on the cross'. To put the matter thus is more than a fanciful figure of speech. I have on my desk as I write a blurred print. It is a photograph taken in a war-zone—it doesn't matter which. It is a picture of a boy, perhaps ten years old, tied to a cross. He is a hungry boy. He has been strung-up as a punishment because he stole some food. This child in this picture is literally on a cross, but he is one with all those other 'children on the cross'—there because that is where, by our neglect or cruelty, we have hanged them.

Our autobiographies of childhood chronicle much pain and distress. It is the hurting child whom Jesus sets in the midst of his disciples. Two contemporary scholars, architects of the 'Child Theology' movement, offer us a radical rereading of the text telling us how Jesus placed a child at the centre of his nascent church. Haddon Willmer and Keith White claim that 'the child in the midst' bears silent witness to the call to take up the cross. I take Willmer and White to be telling us that there, at the centre of the nascent church, is, as it were, the *crucified* child (Willmer and White, 2013).

Much of our ministry among young children is at risk of 'infantilising infants', such is our relentless determination to make and keep them happy. But the children we meet in our homes, schools, and churches are no different from the children we have met in these pages. Many of them are children as 'acquainted with grief' as any saint suffering the soul's night. It is contemptuous of such children to suppose that all they need is entertainment, merry songs, jolly stories, and all that makes much adult involvement with children in today's churches so shallow and frivolous. Children ask of us the space and means whereby they can bring their darkness to the light. And if their darkness lingers it is there in that darkness we must meet and stay with them.

As we do so we are drawn closer to the suffering Christ. We have been brought in this study to a place we did not expect to come to, to the location we might dare to call 'the Calvary of childhood'. The accounts of afflicted childhood we have cited embolden us to suggest that this is not too absurd a place-name. We may struggle to comprehend the darkness Christ entered on the cross. If so, there are the memories of Kathleen Raine, who knew how 'the light itself was emptied of light', to help us.

The importance and significance of the natural world to those children fortunate enough to have experienced it has been the fourth theme of this essay (Chapter Five). Many of the children we have met lived nearer to nature than most children in the west do today. The latter do not have the permission to go out and play. Nor, alas, do they have much inclination to do so. Our children internalise parental fears, both their justified anxieties and their irrational phobias. And anyway they have the latest computer game to get on with. (They do things differently in the Scandinavian countries, still much more outdoor societies.)

In pursuing this project we have looked together at many accounts of out-of-doors childhoods. Most have been of childhoods of earlier generations and there is a risk of misleading mists of nostalgia descending, for not all of those childhoods were happy. Nevertheless, when we read about those 'outdoor children', when in imagination we ramble through the woods and fields with them, we are made aware of the spiritual deprivation our contemporary 'indoor children' suffer.

This essay was written in Britain. A group of academics, writing in the Daily Telegraph, recently claimed that Great Britain 'has the lowest levels of children's well-being in the developed world' (*The Daily Telegraph*, 24th September 2011, 25). Of course there is more to spiritual health than getting plenty of fresh air. But the severance from the sustaining natural order that most western children suffer is immeasurably injurious. Our study leads us to conclude that no task is more urgently necessary for the spiritual nurture of our indoor children than that of reuniting them with the natural world. For the saving of their spirits they must be let out to play.

Throughout these pages I have worked with a rough and ready working description—not a definition—of 'spirituality'. I have suggested that our spirituality is our 'awareness of the other and the beyond'. That awareness is, it seems, acute in children. The evidence of our memoirs—those, at least, that evoke the child's inner experience rather than merely describing the world around them—is that children are in touch with the transcendent. Some children, the 'spiritually gifted' perhaps, seem exceptionally sensitive to an order beyond that ordinarily known. Some experience ecstatic moments amounting to visionary states. Young children do not have the words to talk about such experiences and, later, when words are at their bidding, they are shy of speaking of them.

We are all the more in debt to our writers for sharing their memories of such peak moments of their childhood. We are indebted to them because they do not hide such memories, and we are indebted to them because they are able to find the words to describe them that fail the rest of us.

Memories of such 'peak experiences' were the fifth topic of our study (Chapter Six). I draw attention to three features of these recollections which illuminate the character of the child's spirituality. First such experiences are formative. Specifically, they are *morally* formative. We saw that Maxim Gorky claimed that 'at such moments character is moulded' (Gorky, 1961, 163) and that for A. L. Rowse those moments remained 'a touchstone' and 'an inner resource and consolation' (Rowse, 1942, 85). Rowse claimed that his experience was akin to Wordsworth's for whom such 'intimations of immortality' supplied the 'master-light', the light in which alone can all else be truly seen. (Rowse's appeal to Wordsworth, made by many of our writers, comes as a summons to 'the further work to be done' that Wordsworth sets any who wish to take the investigation of 'the spirituality of recalled childhood' further. Someone soon must settle down to a serious study of Wordsworth's understanding of the spirituality of childhood.)

Secondly, none of those who share with us their memories of these peak experiences give a reductionist account of them. Not one of them suggests that the child's experience was 'nothing more than' an exceptional mental event—an unusual chemical reaction in the brain, some sort of 'high', say, exciting at the time but of no lasting consequence. On the contrary, their understanding of these rare moments is never a matter of 'nothing more' but always a matter of 'much more'. Our writers would insist that there is more—far more—to these experiences than any clinical analysis of them might provide, however sufficient, in its own terms, such an analysis might be. For writers such as Paul Ashton or Richard Church, to name but two of our witnesses, these experiences constitute *disclosures*. They are in some way *revelatory*, however hard it is for the child, or for the adult who recalls the experience, to put into words what is disclosed or revealed.

Thirdly, we register the testimony of Elisaveta Fen who cries to the trees 'I love you'—and then adds, 'I knew I was heard.' For this child there is a *relational* dimension to her ecstatic experience. The peak moments we have shared in this study are places of meeting. For some children at such moments that meeting amounts to a meeting with God. Anne Treneer mistook the splendour she witnessed on Dodman Point for God—except, dare we say, that she was not mistaken (Treneer, 1944, 39-40).

I have suggested that those who seek the spiritual well-being of children entrusted to them must take entirely seriously the possibility that Jesus meant what he said—again we turn to this cardinally important text—when he spoke of things hidden from adults and revealed to children (Matthew 11.25-26). The child who is not listening to what we are saying may be attending instead to that of which we, spiritually short-sighted adults, are unaware.

Grown-ups have mixed memories of their experience of religion. A major theme of this essay, and a sixth topic which we discussed over two chapters (Chapters Seven and Eight), has been the complicated relationship in childhood of religion and spirituality. Too often religion has poisoned fresh wells or, to change the image, clipped fledgling wings. But some of our writers had happier stories to share, of young spirits taking flight, borne aloft by experiences of religion that they look back on with gratitude, whether or not they continued in faith or returned to faith in adult years.

Three major principles emerged from our readings on religion and the spirit. We saw that religion serves the spirit of the child when it affirms and appeals to the child's senses. (Such a lofty generalisation can readily be earthed. Small children find chairs uncomfortable and they should not be made to perch on them.) I suggested that an approach to the nurture of children in the church that has fully recognised and consistently implemented this principle is that of 'Godly Play'. In a Godly Play lesson children are invited to handle simple things that have been beautifully and lovingly made. These *thaumasia* are wonderful—wonderful in themselves, in that they immediately prompt delight, and wonderful too in that they serve the story being told, a open-ended story posing the kind of wondering questions that all of us, children and adults alike, must go on asking if we are to grow in spirit.

We saw, secondly, that the child's spirit will not be served by a religion whose representatives the child has every reason to dislike. We remember 'the furtive she-evangelist, Miss Crouch'. But the problem for the spiritually sensitive child may be less the personal unattractiveness of the teacher than the objectionable nature of what he or she teaches. A sure sign of the awakening spirit is awareness of the morally repugnant. Paul Ashton was taught by his Brethren elders that, unless 'saved', every descendant of Adam and Eve fell with them and was doomed to the fires of hell. Ashton writes,

'I could never accept the justice of that, even when very young. Why would a loving God want to send me, my wonderful hard-smoking unbelieving grandfathers and uncountable millions of other fellow human beings to Hell for something that happened thousands of years before we were born, if indeed it happened at all? (Ashton, 2013, 125)

By contrast the spirit of the child soars when nurtured and nourished by loving adults in whom the child senses a spirit as ardent as his or her own. We recall with joy Percy Lubbock's grandfather. And we shall never forget Maxim Gorky's grandmother playing—*playing*—with her icons.

We saw, thirdly, that children need a language if they are to grow spiritually. Language was our final theme and the subject of the ninth chapter of this study. Many a language may allow the spirit a voice, though no child should be expected to speak several at once. If in our own day many children fail to flourish spiritually that may well be because they are presented with conflicting and competing spiritual languages. Moreover, not all languages lend a healthy voice to the spirit—witness the malign seductions of many a website. The presupposition of this essay has been that the account of things recorded and expressed in the Christian language speaks well of the transcendent—although I trust that I have paid every respect to other languages bearing witness to the beyond. Here again 'the findings' of this study—if they may be so dignified—resonate with the aim of Godly Play, a programme that seeks to enable the child to 'speak Christian'. Needless to say—or perhaps not needless to say—it matters very much that the Christian language be well-spoken. Children both deserve and need teachers who do not 'speak Christian' badly, whose words do not grate on the ear. Far too little attention is given to the sound of what we say to children. It matters less in the child's earliest years that our words make immediate sense than that, already by their very music, they ring true.

Is there one lesson more fundamental than any other these 'remembered childhoods' have taught us? Perhaps there is. We began this study with a rough and ready description of spirituality as 'our awareness of the other and beyond'. We have met children in these pages who felt a hunger for 'something more', a longing, sensed long before words could speak of it, for a realm beyond that of immediate experience. We think of little Helen Forrester, for whom the other side of the Mersey became an image of her true spiritual home. We recall the slum child Richard Roberts hearing in the sound of the ships' sirens a signal beckoning him to 'some fair Hesperides'. We hear the child Rabindranath Tagore echoing in his heart the cry to the ferryman at the river bank 'Take me across'. Some of our writers maintain that this 'other country' beyond the river is somewhere they have already known. The Belfast boy Forrest Reid suffered an aching nostalgia for an Eden from which he knew he was permanently exiled. Even as a child Kathleen Raine felt that she was 'of another race and kind' and that her life was a long return journey to the paradise whence she came. All of which, of course, is pure Wordsworth, but these little children knew what Wordsworth was talking about long before they had read him.

Such children—so they claimed in later years—sensed what the poet Henry Vaughan called 'shadows of eternity' (*The Retreat*). We may dismiss their alleged memories as simply false, as the invention of grown-ups ill at ease with adult life. Or we may see them as the odd moods of hardly normal children. Or we may choose to believe—as I do—that these children saw truly, recognising that of which they could only later speak, that our human condition is ultimately one of estrangement, that we are all natives of another land. If that be so spiritual nurture should not be arduous, for both teacher and taught are going with the grain of all that is. Together we are heading home.

The unending quest

My purpose in this study has been that so memorably expressed by Frank Kendon, 'to wrestle with the angel of childhood till he tells me his secret, and then to put that down, truthfully, for a particular addition to the joy of the world'. The secret that Frank Kendon and his fellow writers sought to penetrate still eludes us. The mystery of childhood remains a mystery. That is not to say that their search and ours has been wasted. Most of the great quests of life are unending but that is no reason for abandoning them. Unending adventures are far from unavailing. Much of worth can be found in fields which hide still greater treasures. I hope that this essay has at least shown that those studying the spirituality of childhood will find autobiographies of childhood a field well worth searching—worth searching for what it tells us about the children we were, the children we are to nurture, and the children we must become. It is ground that has been little explored and one to which I hope others will return.

BIBLIOGRAPHY

The memoirs of childhood referred to in this study are highlighted in bold.

Acland, Eleanor. *Goodbye for the Present: the story of two childhoods.* London: Hodder and Stoughton, 1935.

Adam, Edmond (Juilette Lamber). *The Romance of my childhood and youth.* London: William Heinemann, 1903.

Adams, Kate. *Unseen Worlds: looking through the lens of childhood.* London: Jessica Kingsley. 2010.

Aksakoff, Serghei. *Years of Childhood.* London: OUP, 1923.

Allinson, Francesca. *A Childhood.* London: Hogarth Press, 1937.

Anand, Mulk Raj. *Seven Summers: the Story of an Indian childhood.* London: Penguin, 2005.

Ashton, Paul. *A Puritan at Les Baux.* London: Bell Buoy, 2013.

Austin, Mary. *Experiences Facing Death.* London: Rider & Co, 1931.

Bailey, Paul. *An Immaculate Conception: scenes from childhood and beyond.* London: Penguin, 1990.

Beer, Patricia. *Mrs Beer's House.* London: Hutchinson, 1978.

Benjamin, Walter. *Berlin Childhood around 1900.* Cambridge MA: Belknap Press of Harvard University Press, 2006.

Berryman, Jerome W. *The Spiritual Guidance of Children: Montessori, Godly Play, and the future.* New York: Morehouse, 2013.

Betjeman, John. *Summoned by Bells.* London: John Murray, 1960.

Bjarnhof, Karl. *The Stars grow Pale.* London: Penguin, 1960.

Blake, Bridget. *Bridget's Book: memories of a Falklands childhood.* Stanley, Falkland Islands: The Alastair Cameron Memorial Trust, 2002.

Blishen, Edward. *Sorry, Dad.* London: Hamish Hamilton, 1978.

Boston, L. M. *Perverse and Foolish: a memoir of childhood and youth.* London: Bodley Head, 1979.

Bowlby, John. *Attachment: Attachment and Loss Vol. I.* London: Hogarth Press, 1969.

----*Separation: Anxiety & Anger: Attachment and Loss Vol. 2* London: Hogarth Press, 1973.

----*Loss: Sadness & Depression. Attachment and Loss Vol. 3* London: Hogarth Press, 1980.

Buechner, Frederick. *The Sacred Journey: A memoir of early days*. New York: HarperCollins, 1982.

Burns, D. R. Early *Promise*. Sydney: Alpha Books, 1975.

Chesterton, G. K. *Charles Dickens*. London: Wordsworth Editions, 2007.

Church, Richard. *Over the Bridge: an essay in autobiography*. London: Heinemann, 1955.

Clemenger, Michael. *Everybody Knew. A Boy. Two Brothers. A Stolen Childhood*. London: Random House, 2012.

Coe, Richard. *When the Grass was Taller*. New Haven: Yale University Press, 1984.

Conway, Jill Ker. *The Road from Coorain*. London: Vintage, 1998.

Craig, Patricia. *Bookworm: a memoir of childhood reading*. Co.Cork: Somerville Press, 2015.

Cresswell, Helen. *A Game of Catch*. London: Chatto, Boyd & Oliver, 1969.

Crossley-Holland, Kevin. *The Hidden Roads*. London: Quercus, 2009.

Cuhiddy, Mikey. *A Conversation about Happiness: the story of a lost childhood*. London: Atlantic Books, 2014.

Dall. Ian. *Sun before Seven*. London: Thomas Nelson, 1936.

de Caussade, Jean Pierre. *Abandonment to Divine Providence*. Exeter: Sydney Lee. 1921.

de la Mare, Walter. *Early One Morning*. London: Faber & Faber, 1935.

Dennis, Geoffrey. *Till Seven*. London: Eyre and Spottiswoode, 1957.

Dillard, Annie. *An American Childhood*. London: Picador, 1987.

Donaldson, Frances. *Child of the Twenties*. London: Rupert Hart-Davis, 1959.

Dyment, Clifford. *The Railway Game: an early autobiography*. London: Dent, 1962.

Elias, Eileen. *On Sundays We Wore White*. London: W .H. Allen, 1978.

Enright, D.J. *The Terrible Shears: scenes from a twenties childhood*. London: Chatto & Windus, 1973.

Fedden, Robin. *Chantemesle: a Normandy childhood*. London: John Murray, 1964.

Fen, Elisaveta. *A Russian Childhood*. London: Methuen, 1961.

Fitz-Simon, Christopher. *Eleven Houses: a memoir of childhood*. London: Penguin, 2007.

Flexner, Helen Thomas. *A Quaker Childhood*. New Haven: Yale University Press, 1940.

Forrester, Helen. *Twopence to Cross the Mersey*. Jonathan Cape, London: 1974.

Frank, Anne. *The Diary of a Young Girl*. New York: Doubleday, 1952.

Gandy, Ida. *A Wiltshire Childhood*. London: George Alllen & Unwin, 1929.

Garnett, Angelica. *Deceived with Kindness: A Bloomsbury childhood*. Oxford: Oxford University Press, 1984.

Geisel, Theodor (Dr Seuss). *The Cat in the Hat*. London: Random House, 1957.

Glasser, Ralph. *Growing up in the Gorbals*. London: Chatto and Windus, 1986.

Gosse, Edmund. *Father and Son*. London: Penguin, 1983.

Goodland, Norman. *Sexton's Boy*. London: John Baker, 1967.

Gorky, Maxim, *Childhood*. London: Oxford University Press, 1961.

Graham, R. G. *The Singing Days*. London: Robert Hale, 1961.

Gross, John. *A Double Thread*. London: Chatto & Windus, 2001.

Guppy, Shusha. *The Blindfold Horse: memories of a Persian childhood*. London: Heinemann, 1988.

Hamilton, Elizabeth. *An Irish Childhood*. London: Chatto and Windus, 1963.

Hannam, Charles. *A Boy in your Situation*. London: Andre Deutsch, 1977.

Haworth, Don. *Figures in a Bygone Landscape*. London: Methuen, 1986.

Hay, David. *Something There*, London: Darton, Longman and Todd, 2006.

Hay, David and Nye, Rebecca. *The Spirit of the Child*. London: Fount, 1998 (revised edition: London: Jessica Kingsley, 2006).

Heaney, Seamus. *Mankeepers and Mosscheeper. In Great Irish Stories of Childhood*, Edited by Peter Haining. London: Barnes & Noble, 1997.

Hillen, Ernest. *The Way of a Boy: A Memoir of Java*. London, Penguin, 1995.

Hillyer, Richard. *Country Boy*. London: Hodder and Stoughton, 1966.

Howe, Bea. *Child in Chile*. London: Andre Deutsch, 1957.

Hudson, W.H. *Far Away and Long Ago*, London: J. M. Dent and Sons, 1931.

Hussein, Taha. *An Egyptian Childhood*. London: Routledge, 1932.

Ivaldi, Jeanne. *Who will watch over me? A childhood memoir*. London: Cromwell Publishers, 2001.

Jefferies, Richard. *Bevis, the Story of a Boy*, London: Jonathan Cape, 1932.

-----*The Story of my Heart: my Autobiography*. London: Longmans Green, 1883.

----*Wood Magic*, Longmans Green, 1881.

Joyce, James. *Portrait of the Artist as a Young Man*. Ware: Wordsworh Editions, 1992.

Kendon, Frank. *The Small Years*. Cambridge: Cambridge University Press, 1950.

Kirkup, James. *The Only Child: an Autobiography of Infancy*. London: Collins, 1957.

---- Sorrows, *Passions, and Alarms*. London: Collins, 1959.

Lakeman, Mary. *Early Tide: A Mevagissey childhood*. London: William Kimber, 1978.

Laye, Camara. *The African Child*. London: 1959.

Lee, Laurie. *Cider with Rosie*. London: Penguin, 1962.

Lewis, C. S. *Surprised by Joy*. London: Fontana, 1959.

Lewis, C. S. *Transposition and Other Addresses*. London: Geoffrey Bles, 1949.

Lewis, Eiluned. *Dew on the Grass*. London: Peter Davies, 1934.

Litvinoff, Emanuel. *Journey through a Small Planet*. London: Robin Clark, 1993.

Lively, Penelope. *Oleander, Jacaranda*. London: Penguin, 1995.

Lubbock, Percy. *Earlham*. London: Jonathan Cape, 1922.

---- *Shades of Eton*, London: Jonathan Cape, 1929.

MacCarthy, Mary. *Memories of a Catholic Girlhood*. London: Penguin, 1963.

McCourt, Frank. *Angela's Ashes*. London: Flamingo, 1997.

Magan, William. *An Irish Boyhood*. Edinburgh: Pentland Press, 1996.

Magee, Bryan. *Clouds of Glory: a Hoxton childhood*. London: Jonathan Cape, 2003.

Markino, Yoshio. *When I was a Child*. London: Constable, 1912.

Masefield, John. *So Long to Learn*. London: Heinemann, 1952.

Maslow, Abraham, *Religions, Values, and Peak Experience*. London: Penguin, 1994.

Matane, Paulias. *My Childhood in New Guinea*. Oxford: Oxford University Press, 1972.

Motion, Andrew. *In the Blood: a memoir of my childhood*. London: Faber and Faber, 2006.

Murry, Colin Middleton. *One Hand Clapping: a memoir of childhood*. London: Victor Gollancz, 1975.

Nielsen, Carl. *My Childhood*. London: Hutchinson, London, 1953.

O'Connor, Frank. *An Only Child*. London: Penguin. 2005.

Paffard, Michael. *The Unattended Moment*. London: SCM, 1976.

Pearson. W. W., and Dey, M. C. *Shantiniketan: the Bolpur school of Rabindranath Tagore*, London: Macmillan, 1916.

Paul, Leslie. *The Living Hedge*. London: Faber and Faber, 1946.

Paustovsky, Konstantin. *Story of a Life: childhood and schooldays*. London: Harvill, 1964.

Pemba, Tsewang Y. *Young Days in Tibet*. London: Jonathan Cape, 1957.

Porter, Hal. *The Watcher on the Cast-iron Balcony*. London: Faber, 1963.

Raine, Kathleen. *Farewell Happy Fields*. London: Hamish Hamilton, 1973.

Raverat, Gwen. *Period Piece*. London: Faber, 1960.

Raynor, John. *A Westminster Childhood*. London: Cassell, 1973.

Read, Herbert, *Annals of Innocence and Experience*. London: Faber and Faber, 1946.

Reid, Forrest. *Apostate*, London: Constable, Faber, 1947.

Roberts, Robert. *A Ragged Schooling: Growing up in a classic slum*. Manchester: Manchester University Press, 1976.

Rousseau, *Emile*. London: Dent, 1911.

Rowse, A. L. *A Cornish Childhood*. London: Jonathan Cape, 1942.

Rutherford, Dorothea. *The Threshold: A memoir of childhood*. London: Rupert Hart-Davis, 1955.

Sircar, Noel. *An Indian Boyhood*. London: Hollis and Carter, 1948.

Slater, Nigel. *Toast: the story of a boy's hunger*. London: Fourth Estate, 2003.

Smith, Bertram. *Running Wild.* London: Simpkin, Marshall, Hamilton, Kent, 1920.

Smith, Emma. *The Great Western Beach: A memoir of a Cornish childhood between the wars.* London: Bloomsbury, 2008.

Soskice, Juliet M. *Chapters from Childhood: reminiscences of an artist's granddaughter.* New York: Turtle Point Press, 1994.

Sutcliff, Rosemary. *Blue Remembered Hills: A recollection.* Oxford: Oxford University Press, 1984.

Tagore, Rabindranath. *Gitanjali.* London: Macmillan, 1913a.

---- *Sādhāna: the realisation of life.* London: Macmillan, 1913b.

---- *Reminiscences.* London:, Macmillan, 1917.

---- *The Religion of Man,* London: George Allen & Unwin, 1931.

Tagore, R. and Elmhirst, L. K. *Rabindranath Tagore: pioneer in education,* John Murray, 1961.

Thompson, Brian. *Keeping Mum.* London: Atlantic Books, 2006.

Thompson, Nancy. *At Their Departing: a childhood memoir.* London: Hamish Hamilton, 1986.

Tolstoy, Leo. *Childhood, Boyhood, and Youth.* London: Oxford University Press. 1930.

Traherne, Thomas. *Centuries.* London: The Faith Press, 1960.

Tregenza, Leo. *Harbour Village: yesterday in Cornwall.* London: William Kimber, 1977.

Treneer, Anne. *School House in the Wind.* London: Jonathan Cape, 1944.

Uttley, Alison. *The Country Child.* London: Nelson 1936.

Vaughan, Paul. *Something in Linoleum: a thirties education.* London: Sinclair-Stevenson, 1994.

Walker, Ted. *The High Path.* London: Routledge and Kegan Paul, 1982.

Walsh, Marrie. *An Irish Country Childhood.* London: Metro, 2010.

White, Antonia. *Frost in May.* London: Eyre & Spottiswoode, 1933.

White, Peter. *Seeing it my Way,* Little, Brown & Company, 1999

Wigger, J. Bradley. "See-through Knowing: learning from children and their invisible friends." *Journal of Childhood and Religion* 2.3(2011), 1-34.

Willmer, Haddon & White, Keith. *Entry Point: Towards Child Theology with Matthew 18.* London: WTL Publications, 2013.

Wollheim, Richard. *Germs: A Memoir of Childhood*. London: Waywiser, 2004.

Woodruff, William, *The Road to Nab End: A Lancashire Childhood*. London: Eland, 2011.

Woolf, Leonard. *Sowing*. London: Hogarth Press 1962.

Woolf, Virginia. *Moments of Being*. London: Grafton Books, 1989.

Yust, Karen-Marie. "Digital Power: exploring the effects of social media on children's spirituality." *International Journal of Children's Spirituality* 19(2) (2014), 133-143.

CPSIA information can be obtained
at www.ICGtesting.com
Printed in the USA
LVOW03s0017270717
542739LV00001B/84/P